GOD T
SOFTLY

Trevor Dennis started preaching through storytelling in the 1970s, when he was a school chaplain, but most of his pieces since, including the ones contained in this book, have been designed primarily for adults. For nearly twelve years he taught Old Testament studies at Salisbury and Wells Theological College, and then in 1994 joined the staff of Chester Cathedral, where he is Vice Dean. This is his fifth collection of stories and meditations published by SPCK, his earlier ones being *Speaking of God* (1992), *Imagining God* (1997), *The Three Faces of Christ* (1999) and *Keeping God Company* (2002). SPCK has also published four other books of his, exploring examples of the storytelling and poetry of the Old Testament. His most recent book is a children's Bible, published by Lion in 2003, and he is a regular contributor to the Bible Reading Fellowship's *Guidelines* series of Bible notes. He is married to Caroline, who teaches dyslexic children, and they have four children and one grandson. He is also a keen birdwatcher.

GOD TREADS
SOFTLY HERE

Trevor Dennis

First published in Great Britain in 2004 by
SPCK
Holy Trinity Church
Marylebone Road
London NW1 4DU

British Library Cataloguing-in-Publication Data
A catalogue record for this book is available from the British Library

ISBN 0-281-05655-2

1 3 5 7 9 10 8 6 4 2

Typeset by Pioneer Associates, Perthshire
Printed in Great Britain by
Bookmarque Ltd, Croydon, Surrey

CONTENTS

CONTENTS

INTRODUCTION

There is much in the Christian tradition and in the Bible itself to encourage us to speak of an exclusive God, a God who chooses one and rejects another. Yet there is also a great deal in both Scripture and tradition to point us towards a God whose love is large enough to embrace the entire universe, let alone our flawed humanity, and whose readiness to forgive passes our understanding. Such an inclusive God does not just belong to the Bible and the teaching of the Church, but to experience, to the experience of countless men, women and children. I count myself among them. Such is the God I know. I know of no other.

I have been preaching such a God for very many years, sometimes through storytelling or poetry, where the story or the poem forms the whole sermon, without further elaboration or attempt to elucidate. Four collections of my pieces have already been published by SPCK, and this little book constitutes the fifth. Most of the pieces were preached in Chester Cathedral, where I am on the staff. I am very grateful to SPCK for showing such a surprising and persistent interest in my work, and especially to Alison Barr, my editor, for her encouragement (what stamina!), her perceptiveness and her great care.

The pieces in this book, like those in my earlier collections, draw on a wealth of biblical material, but an unusual number of them pay special heed to three parables of Jesus: the Lost Sheep, the Lost Coin, and the Prodigal Son. That is a mark of how those parables have recently come to life for me once again. Many commentators argue they take us to the heart of

Jesus of Nazareth. In that case, since we Christians believe that Jesus shows us God, they take us close to the very heart of God.

The moment in the Prodigal Son when the younger son returns and the father runs to meet him is surely one of the most powerful in all Scripture, and you will find it keeps cropping up in the pieces in this book. However, in one respect the Parables of the Lost Sheep and Lost Coin are even more audacious in their depiction of the forgiveness and love of God, for the lost sheep, unlike the prodigal son, does not turn back towards the shepherd, but remains hopelessly lost until it is found, while the coin can do nothing but lie there in the dirt.

We are familiar with the image of God as the good shepherd. It is an ancient metaphor, and is found in various places in the Old Testament, as well as in John's Gospel or the Parable of the Lost Sheep itself. For all its familiarity, it remains an inspiring one, and some of the pieces in this collection bear witness to the way it has moved and challenged me. The picture of God as a peasant housewife, anxiously searching for her lost treasure, is far less common, and it took me a very long time, well over fifty years indeed, to wake up to it and feel its force. Yet there it was, staring me in the face all along, in the Parable of the Lost Coin.

Where did that woman keep her ten coins? The parable doesn't tell us. What would Jesus himself and his audience have imagined? Some commentators have suggested they would have seen them adorning her headdress, but others have explained that a woman from a Palestinian village would have had them about her neck. I like that idea! Oh, I am aware of yet more commentators who tell me the particular coins indicated by the original Greek of the text would have been too small to pierce and hang upon a string, but the image of ourselves belonging to God's necklace is so extraordinary and so precious, that I can't let it go. And what if we imagine the coins against her 'skin'? Palestinian women in Jesus' day would have worn their jewellery on the outside of their clothing, but my wife, like most contemporary western women, often wears a necklace next to her skin. We belong to God's precious necklace, and are truly at home when we find ourselves touching her skin! That is what I find myself thinking and feeling when I hear the Parable of the Lost Coin. It is far too daring an image for the pages of careful doctrine. It belongs instead to the language of playful storytelling and poetry, a language which sometimes has the miraculous power to conjure up an elusive, mysterious God and bring her very close.

So against her skin it is!

That is only one example of the freedom I have sometimes exercised in these pieces in my handling of the biblical text. I have, for example, made Moses' wife Zipporah deaf, and imagined her and Moses going up to the top of Mount Sinai as contemporary pilgrims. I have spoken of Jesus being given a hurried burial by the soldiers who had crucified him. You might protest, 'But it didn't happen like that!' And I would agree at once, of course, that that is not how the story is told in the Bible. But then I would say, 'Don't worry about it. My story says something else. I'm not trying to compete with the Bible (as if anyone could). I'm simply allowing the storytelling and poetry of the Bible (and remember, that's what it is, not a journalistic record of events) to work on my imagination and my prayer, mixing in my experience and study, and then responding in my own way. That's all.'

There is a real sense in which anything we say about God is a nonsense. What I say about God in this book is a nonsense. But I hope it might be entertaining nonsense, moving and challenging nonsense, which by some miracle of God's doing draws you deeper into the strange, yet wonderful territory of God's love.

TREVOR DENNIS
Chester Cathedral

FOR GOD'S SAKE DO IT PROPERLY!

These lines were composed for a service in Chester Cathedral in Advent 2002, when talk of a 'flood' of asylum seekers was dominating much of the news in Britain, yet more terrible stories were coming out of Bethlehem (it has got still worse there since) and the memories of 9/11 remained as vivid as ever in our minds. I make clear use of Paul's wonderful poem on love in 1 Corinthians 13 and of the Parable of the Prodigal Son in Luke 15.

This time, God,
for God's sake do it properly!
No messing about,
none of that self-effacing stuff.
We've had enough of your shyness,
your doing things in out-of-the-way places.
Who'd ever heard of Nazareth?
And Bethlehem was not much better,
no Jerusalem, that's for sure,
let alone another Rome.

This time, God,
walk the corridors of power!
London this time, not Bethlehem,
Washington, instead of Nazareth.
Walk the walk,
talk the talk,
put some swagger into it!
And bring the legions of angels with you.

Be decisive, God,
like you were at the Flood.
That was showing them!
(Why did you promise never to do it again?)
Things were desperate then,
the earth all ruined,
you said so yourself.

Well, *our* chickens are coming home to roost, they say.
We're beginning to pay the price
for our pride, our greed and our complacency, apparently.
Tens of thousands flocking to our shores
for a bit of what we've got,
and hundreds of thousands behind them.
The tabloids are going bonkers,
and the Government's strutting about and talking tough,
yet still they come,
not knowing we have so nearly lost our soul.

Then there are the schemers, the plotters and the bombers:
planes hammered into buildings,
bus-loads of children blown to kingdom come,
and holy places spattered with blood.
The soldiers are back in your precious Bethlehem,
killing the children again,
and leaving bedridden old women
hanging in houses half battered to the ground.

Oh, and the deserts are growing,
and the ice-caps melting;
AIDS makes orphans every minute of the year,
while tight-lipped hunger takes too many of the rest.

And we ourselves have fled to cynicism, or denial, or both.

So this time, God,
for God's sake do it properly!

    For my sake,
    or for yours?

    I did it properly the first time,
    the only way I know.

    I only know the ways of love,
    and love casts out all fear,
    won't have it in the house.
    Love has no swagger,
    stands on no ceremony
    draws no attention to itself,
    is not loud, nor bombastic,
    never puts anyone down;
    love builds up, renews, restores,
    gently, patiently,
    never giving up,
    never yielding to despair,
    never cynical,
    always new,
    always surprising,
    quite unbreakable.

    I play the waiting game.
    When you play prodigal,
    I do not follow you,
    spy on you,
    drag you out of the mire,
    haul you by the hair to where you belong.
    I simply wait.

But give me the slightest chance,
just a glimpse of your turning,
and I will run to embrace you
and give you a homecoming
beyond your wildest dreams.

And then you will be freed from your complacency,
your pride and your nagging greed,
and you will find again your soul,
to give others back their dignity
and my good earth its beauty.

Do not keep me waiting for too long.

ROOM FOR GOD TO LIVE

Thou' hast light in darke; and shutst in little roome,
Immensity cloystered in thy deare wombe.

(Lines from John Donne's sonnet, 'Annunciation', part of
a short cycle of poems reflecting on the birth, death and
resurrection of Jesus, entitled *La Corona*.)

O Mary, you are not the only place
where God is so contained.
Go down from Nazareth to Jerusalem
and you will find him there
locked in a cupboard;
and only the High Priest has the key.

All is grandeur in Jerusalem, Mary,
Herod's grandeur of gold and fine-hewn stone,
grandeur designed to keep the likes of you at bay.
In Jerusalem you will not get past the Court of the
    Women, Mary,
and the Holy of Holies is utterly beyond you,
for you are too poor, Mary,
too ignorant, too female.

Yet here you are,
(little do they know in Jerusalem),
with God shut in the little room of your belly!
It is a miracle, Mary.
There is no other word for it.

Little do they know in Jerusalem
how they have imprisoned God
behind their smoking paraphernalia,
behind the bars of that famous curtain
across their innermost sanctuary.
Little do they know
how one day that same curtain will be ripped apart
and God will escape from their religion,
like a man leaving behind his tomb
and the tight wrappings of his death.

Your womb is no imprisonment, Mary.
God will need to leave it, certainly,
to learn to smile and laugh and walk
and tell outrageous tales
and play his shepherd's pipe
and sing the truth.
For now it is enough for him
to grow inside you,
to put on fingers, toes
and smooth brown skin
and eyes as dark as olives,
to learn to suck his thumb and kick.

Yet still – oh Mary! – we build our temples
where we lock God in to die.
Oh teach us, Mary,
to give dear God a little room in which to live!

3

HE BEGAN SO SMALL

*This piece ranges widely through the Gospels, from Matthew's
story of the birth of Jesus, the escape to Egypt, and the massacre
of the babies of Bethlehem (Matthew 2), to the Parable of the
Lost Coin (Luke 15.8–9), the Parable of the Good Samaritan
(Luke 10.25–37), Jesus' meeting with the Samaritan woman
in John 4, with Legion in Mark 5, and Zacchaeus in Luke 19,
and to some of the events of the Passion.*

He began so small,
curled in the pulsing dark
of the womb of a girl
frightened one morning by an angel,
finding herself prematurely breathing heaven.
He was safe there,
guarded against the girl's poverty,
with just enough for his growing,
oblivious to her threatening disgrace,
warmed by her defiance.
He sensed the quickening of her heart,
when she told the news of his small presence
and hid behind her mother's skirts
against the shocked rage of her father,
but that was all.

And when he was new-born,
he only felt the smooth skin of her breast,
her milk, sucking sweet,

the look in her eyes
and her safe holding,
and Joseph's gentle calloused hands.
He did not know he had so nearly come between them,
nor the strangeness of their pride
in him, their unexpected child.
He did not know he was a Jew;
the name Herod meant nothing to him;
he did not hear the soldiers marching from Jerusalem.
He was not there for the slaughter,
nor even understood that they had fled
and lost the little they had had.
Home was where his mother was
and where his father's arms were strong.
He was quite at home in Egypt,
nor knew he was an outsider.
He had no prejudice of any kind,
nor hate, nor violence.
He only knew the little world of love.

He never grew up.
That was his trouble
and his downfall.

From his small childhood
he knew a God who played,
who hid herself among the flowers,
or spread her wings to tumble from the stars.
He knew a God who lived next door,
and wore him like a shining coin
against the closeness of her neck.
He only knew her little world of love
and filled with her his universe.

When grown to man, and grown to Jew,
he did not share the sharp distinctions others made.
He did not see that some were worth their weight in gold,
while others hardly counted on the scales.
He laughed with scribe and Pharisee,
told tales of good Samaritans
and came to ask for water from their wells.
Even when he met the Legions of his world
and found the reasons for their madness,
the women raped
the children cut to pieces,
the houses burned
before their very eyes,
he did not learn to hate.
And when the crowd of Jericho
bunched thin shoulders together,
and made Zacchaeus climb a tree,
he still refused to hate,
but honoured him instead
by asking to become his honoured guest.
He cast no stones,
though fields and streets were thick with them,
and others had them ready in their fists.

Put up against the ancient olives of Gethsemane,
he had no sword with which to fight.
When Judas found him with that kiss,
he wished to dress him in the finest robe,
put gleaming shoes upon his feet
and sit him down to fatted calf.
Faced with a High Priest
who thought God could never live next door,
for God was God and far too grand for that,

he told him God would get her broom
and search for him to hang about her neck once more.
Being still God's child
he found unerringly the child curled up
in the dark cupboard of Pilate's cruelty,
held out his arms to hold him tight.
When Pilate pinned those arms to blood-stained wood,
for fear of feeling his embrace,
still, yet still he did not learn to hate.
And when the other bandit taunted him,
he took him too to paradise,
so God could tie her necklace once again.

And still, yet still he knew a God who played,
who hid herself among the flowers,
spread wide her wings to tumble from the stars,
and held us all against her breast
and rocked us in our fear;
he knew her
though he felt she had deserted him
and left him on that wood for dead.

And that is why he holds a mirror to ourselves,
so we can see just who we are;
and that is why he shows us who our neighbour is,
and shows us none is stranger to us,
let alone our enemy,
but all hang close about God's neck.
And that is why he shows us God,
and always will,
and always will.

Love him,
hold him,
bathe his wounds,
take him to an inn,
pay whatever is needed.
Go back with him to Jerusalem.

THE SHEPHERDS

The story of the shepherds' visit to the new-born Jesus in Luke 2 provides the obvious basis for this piece, but there is reference also to the imagery of Job 38—39, and to the story of the wise men in Matthew 2.

1st shepherd	I tell you, we didn't know what we would find at the end of our journey. We thought we knew. We had our expectations.
2nd shepherd	It was not as we thought it would be, and we will never be the same again.
3rd shepherd	We are shepherds, illiterate, of course, and so, by your book, quite unlike the wise men; Bedouin, not Jews, nor Romans, nor anyone that counts; semi-nomadic, living the other side of the fence of what you call civilization. We were the last people you would expect to lead you to the mystery of God.
2nd shepherd	That is why we went on our own.
1st shepherd	Not from the fields below Bethlehem. We came out of the desert, as we always do, knowing we would find God at the end of our journey, but expecting the wrong one.
3rd shepherd	The God we knew lived among us in the desert, searching with us for lost sheep, carrying lambs in his strong arms, playing midwife to the ibex and the antelope, untying the ropes of the stars

to let them pasture in the fields of the night, tilting the waterskins of heaven to make it rain and covering the hills with flowers, soaring with the eagle, turning in the sun with the migrating storks, treading through the silence, and dancing uproariously to our pipes. Our women sometimes came across her at the well, and knew her always at times of birth and death.

2nd shepherd Yet we expected to find the god the clever people spoke of, the god who lived at the end of long corridors of power, where we would never be allowed, or could feel at home if we were, the royal god for whom gifts of gold, frankincense and myrrh would be appropriate.

1st shepherd We had no such gifts to bring, of course. Quite out of our league.

3rd shepherd You might ask why we went at all, if we didn't expect to be allowed near him. Why set out for an inaccessible god, when we had God so close to us in the desert?

1st shepherd We wished to find answers to some old, nagging questions: Had we made our God too parochial? Had we confined our God to the desert and its ways? Was our God of our own making? Was our God too small?

2nd shepherd We thought for a moment he was, when we came in sight of Jerusalem and saw its temple. We had given our God a tent, to mark his presence with us. Not to live in, of course. Our God stretched far beyond the stars, was larger than the desert's silence, deeper than its sand and rock. But we had given him a tent as a mark of our hospitality, to make him feel he belonged, to shelter him against the cold of the night and the heat of the sun.

3rd shepherd   The temple in Jerusalem was not made of goat skins, as our tent was. Had we forgotten the grandeur of God? At first the temple made us think we had. Should we have learned to be afraid of God? The temple made us wonder.

1st shepherd   It made us mighty uncomfortable, too. It lacked generosity. Its god lacked generosity. Our God was free, and had given us the freedom of the desert. This temple-god was surrounded by rules and regulations, the rules of the city, the regulations of powerful men, who used them to lord it over the likes of us.

3rd shepherd   Our women could not imagine meeting that god at the well.

2nd shepherd   So we were relieved when we realized the temple did not mark the end of our journey. We were drawn on, to an out-of-the-way place, to a side street, to a one-roomed house with an animal stall under its roof and a feeding trough on its floor, to a family – the one whose house it was – standing there, grandmother, mother with a baby in her arms, father, six other children, and a young girl exhausted from the pain and terror of giving birth, her man kneeling beside the feeding trough, and a new-born baby, tight wrapped, lying in the straw.

1st shepherd   We felt at home in that place, more at home than we had ever felt before. We were most welcome.

3rd shepherd   They gave us food and drink, of course, the family of the house. Later the entire village came together and put on a feast to mark our coming and the birth of the child. They killed their fatted calf. We sat in a single circle under the stars and ate together, men, women and children. We had never seen anything quite like it before.

2nd shepherd When the child woke up and had been fed and winded, his mother let us hold him, each one of us in turn.

3rd shepherd I can still feel that small weight. It contained all the love of heaven and all earth's hope and longing! Have you ever held God in your arms?

1st shepherd He *was* the God we knew so well, but closer still than we had ever dreamed. Against our cheeks he was! We had feared we had made our God too small. Truth is, we had not made him small enough. He was not as we expected. But then, God never is.

3rd shepherd What would happen when he grew to a man, we wondered, and saw that temple in Jerusalem?

2nd shepherd I still carry God in my arms. When I go down to the wadi with the sheep and the goats, I still carry God in my arms.

3rd shepherd When I climb to the top of that ancient holy mountain I know so well, I carry God in my arms, also, to show him the beauty of his world. We listen together to its silence.

1st shepherd When the soldiers come to humiliate us and keep us waiting in the sun, or ransack our tents, terrify our children and rape our women, I still carry God in my arms and hold him very tight, and find that he is holding me.

2nd shepherd	And when we sit all of us round the fire under the stars, in one single circle, men, women and children together, and eat and drink and tell our tales and play our pipes and lutes and sing and watch the small children dance and catch them when they fall, we still hold God in our arms and bounce him on our knees.
1st, 2nd, *3rd shepherds*	Here, you hold him for a moment.

AN INTERVIEW WITH THE WISE MEN

Matthew's story of the wise men can be found in his Gospel at 2.1–18. We often talk as if the story ends with their offering their gifts and returning home, but, of course, it leads straight into flight and fearful massacre. We must also recall that whereas in Luke's birth stories Mary and Joseph come from Nazareth and travel down to Bethlehem for the birth, Matthew represents Bethlehem as their home village. Matthew does not speak of any other members of their families, but it is perfectly reasonable to imagine they were there.

There was silence in the tent. The wise men were sitting on an exquisite Persian carpet, perfectly still. They seemed uneasy, distracted. The western interviewer was not used to sitting on the floor, and was finding it difficult to make herself comfortable. She wondered whether her gender was a problem. Indeed, she had been surprised when they had agreed to speak to her, particularly in the relative privacy of the tent. From time to time someone brought in more sweet tea for her to drink and small piles of sweet cakes.

The silence was broken by the sounds of a lute and soft singing. One of the three had taken down his lute from a peg, tuned it and started playing and singing. The other two joined in, and soon children appeared at the door of the tent and one of them ran to the lute player and threw herself into his lap. He stopped playing and smiled down at her as she ran her small fingers over the strings. The lilting song continued, and soon the small child was asleep. The man stroked her head.

The other two watched him. All three of them had tears in their eyes.

The lute player spoke first:

1st wise man	Sometimes we wish we hadn't gone.
2nd wise man	Often.
3rd wise man	We were fools.
1st wise man	Naive.
2nd wise man	We'd had our heads too long in our books.

Silence came once more. The child lay fast asleep in the man's arms.

Interviewer	What do you mean? You found what you were searching for. You found God himself. Surely you can have no regrets?
3rd wise man	Do you not know what happened after we left for home?
Interviewer	You mean the slaughter of the children?
1st wise man	The massacre, yes. They were smaller than little Vashti here. We could have prevented it.
Interviewer	By going back to Herod and telling him exactly where he could find Jesus, do you mean? Surely you couldn't have done that?
3rd wise man	No, of course we couldn't. We didn't belong to Herod's secret police. And in any case after we had seen that child, nothing on earth would have made us betray him. If Herod had captured us and tortured us, he wouldn't have got anything out of us.
2nd wise man	But we shouldn't have blundered into Jerusalem asking for the King of the Jews. We should have

asked if they had a king already. Two kings for one throne is one too many. We knew that, of course. But we assumed when we saw this new king's star in its rising that the old king must be dead. We were wrong, quite tragically so.

1st wise man We should have asked more questions first. We should have found out about Herod.

3rd wise man And we shouldn't have been beguiled by the temple he was building. It was the grandest thing we had ever seen. On such a scale! Such fine workmanship! The blocks of stone so finely cut! We had heard tales of Persepolis, once the royal centre of our empire, with its palaces and irrigated gardens. Jerusalem reminded us of those old stories. A palace for its god, set on a huge platform, so that the whole world could come and fall at his feet!

2nd wise man And pay homage to the king who had built it for him.

1st and
3rd wise men Of course.

Interviewer What do you mean the temple 'beguiled' you?

2nd wise man It led us to expect the wrong kind of king, and to think our gifts were appropriate. We had gold and frankincense and myrrh in our saddle bags. We imagined we came as ambassadors from our country, that we came on behalf of the whole Gentile world, indeed. Perhaps that was arrogant of us. We imagined we would find the new king in a splendid court, surrounded by his own wise men, and guarded by soldiers, so we had brought presents fit for a monarch. That was stupid.

1st wise man   Yet not nearly so stupid as the question we asked in the suq in Jerusalem. 'Where is the child who has been born King of the Jews?' we said. 'We saw his star rise in the night sky back in Persia,' we said. 'We set out to follow it, and here we are,' we said. Such fools! Why couldn't we have kept our mouths shut, been more discreet, been more *wise*! The children of Bethlehem would not have died then.

He turned his face away. His tears fell on Vashti's face. Gently he wiped them away with his sleeve.

1st wise man   When, after our audience with Herod . . .

He looked down and shook his head. There was a long silence. Eventually he picked up the story again.

After our audience with Herod we rode the few miles to Bethlehem and found the child king we had come for. Or rather, we found something, someone quite different.

2nd wise man   We had turned our backs on Herod's temple. We found no court, no courtiers, no soldiers at our destination. Instead we found a peasant family's house, with its space for their two animals, and a peasant family's hospitality, and a young girl and her man and a child crying for milk, and a group of shepherds unable to tear themselves away from the door, surrounded by their sheep and goats, and a sky full of angels and the whole of heaven squeezed in amongst it all.

3rd wise man   We were embarrassed about the gifts we had brought. They seemed at first quite out of place, far too grand, far too expensive and exclusive. Yet they were at once accepted. We had brought the finest things we could think of, and they were placed carefully among the gifts of the family, the gifts the rest of the village had brought, the gifts of the shepherds and the children. They too had given their finest things.

1st wise man   We had not found a king at all. We had found God, and that was quite different. We are so glad we went. How could we not be? And yet ...

2nd wise man   The God-child had to escape to Egypt after we had gone. Did you know that? They left their families behind. Did you know that? And did you know that Mary's sister had her own baby, a few weeks old, and Joseph's brother a small boy just starting to walk?

3rd wise man   That is why we and our wives and children now run this orphanage.

The interviewer looked across to the entrance of the tent. The children were still standing there, looking at her.

The first wise man looked across to them and pointed to Vashti sleeping in his arms. Then all three nodded to them, and at once they ran in and flung themselves upon the other two and upon the interviewer till they were quite buried in a giggling heap of small bodies.

Vashti slept through it all.

SO WHAT DID THE CHILDREN
DO IN BETHLEHEM?

Very rarely do we hear in the Bible the experiences of children. I wrote the original version of this piece for a children's Christmas service in Chester Cathedral, and gave my imagination free rein. When, the following Christmas, I used it again, but in the course of a service for adults, I changed a few details and gave it a new ending.

'So what did the children do in Bethlehem, when the angels filled the sky with song and the shepherds came running from the fields, and then, on another day, in another story, wise men arrived to give their gifts? Were they there?'

'Oh yes. They were there.'

'Did they stay on the edge? Did the adults get in the way, as sometimes they do?'

'Not this time. It was crowded, for sure. The shepherds brought all their sheep and goats with them. They couldn't leave them out in the fields, for there were wolves around, and lions, leopards and bears. The sheep and goats would have been easy meat. So they brought them all with them and the place where Jesus was lying got packed out. There wasn't room for a flea! But the children managed to crawl between the legs of the animals and got to the front. They put their faces over the edge of the manger, and they saw him, with their very own eyes they saw him, lying there in the straw.

'It was as quiet as the stars. The sheep and goats didn't make a sound. So when a small boy called Nathan said something, everyone heard him. He was peering over the side of the

—22—

manger and looking right into Jesus' eyes. "I didn't know you looked like that, God," he said.

'Clutched tight in his hand Nathan held a stone, his favourite stone, round and shiny, silver and white and blue and very beautiful, like a great pearl, a pearl of great price. He'd found it one day out in the fields and it was his greatest treasure. No-one knew about it, except him. Even his brother and his baby sister, even his mother and father, even his best friend, didn't know about it. It was his secret, the most precious, the finest thing in all the world. "It's too big for him to swallow," he thought to himself. He knew about babies putting things in their mouths. His sister Rebekah, just a few months old, did it with everything she could lay her hands on. He stood on his toes, stretched his arm over the side of the manger, and slipped the stone into the straw near Jesus' head, where he would be sure to find it.'

⌒◯⌒

'And what happened when the wise men arrived? Were the children there again?'

'Oh, yes. When the wise men got to the village, to Bethlehem, they called the children together.

'"Now," they said, "we're going to have a great procession to see the Christ child, and we want you to lead it. We'll all carry lamps to light our way and we'll weave them around the village like a necklace of stars. We'll take these little stars to the place where Jesus lies, and there we'll stop and ring his house around with light.

'"And when we go inside, we'll sing to him. The shepherds heard some angels sing, so we've heard. And the shepherds have taught you the angels' song. We know that, too. We are very wise men, you see," and their eyes twinkled.

'"So first, before we light our candles, you must teach us

— 23 —

that song, so we can all sing it as we stand round the manger."

'Rachel, one of the girls, spoke up. "If we find him crying," she said, "we can sing it very softly, to soothe him to sleep, and if we find him sleeping, we can sing it in our quietest voices of all, so he can hear the song in his dreams, but we don't wake him up. Whatever we do, we mustn't sing too loud, because babies don't like loud noises. I know that, because I've got a baby brother called Simon, and he doesn't like loud noises, they make him screw up his face and cry."

'"Quite right," the wise men said. "Sing us the song now, Rachel. Sing us a verse, and then the others can join in."

'So Rachel sang, and quite forgot herself. The song filled her head, the angels filled her voice, and she sang as she had never sung before. At last she came to the end of the verse, and waited for the other children to join in with the next one. But they all remained silent, their mouths open, their eyes fixed on her. Suddenly she noticed them looking at her and she turned to the nearest of the wise men, wondering what she'd done wrong. He knelt down in front of her. "You sing for us," he said quietly. "When we get to the Christ child, you sing, just like that."

'And so she did. Jesus was crying when they found him. "We can't seem to do anything to make him stop," Joseph said. "Mary's fed him, so he can't be hungry. And he's warm enough. It's as if he can see things we can't and hear things beyond our hearing; as if he already knows all there is to know, and that is far too much. I know that sounds stupid, but we don't know what to do. Can you say something wise to quieten him down?"

'He was speaking to the wise men. "I don't think we can," they said. "But Rachel will. Only she'll sing it."

'They looked across at her and nodded their heads.

'Rachel began the angels' song, laying the notes gently on

the baby's cries. At first the others could hardly hear her singing, for Jesus' crying was too loud. But gradually it became less and less, while the song grew more and more until it filled the whole space where they were, spilled out into the night air, took up the darkness and flowed over into heaven. Jesus had stopped crying. He was looking at Rachel. He was new-born, so his eyes could not focus, yet he seemed to be looking intently at her. She reached the end of the final verse. A deep silence fell upon the place. No-one moved.

'Nathan was standing by the crib beside Rachel, peering over its side. He was trying to catch a glimpse of his stone amongst the straw, wanting to make sure it was still there safe. He couldn't see it. Then he noticed Jesus was holding something. He stood right on the very tip of his toes and bent his head closer. Yes! He could see his stone poking out from Jesus' hand. "Brilliant!" he whispered.

ᘒᘒ

'In Jerusalem King Herod, his head full of fear, waited for the wise men to return and tell him where the Christ child was, so he could give precise instructions to his men. They never came, so he had to send far more troops into the village than he had planned. Neither Nathan's sister Rebekah nor Rachel's brother Simon survived.'

7

'DO NOT FOLLOW ME. MY DAY IS OVER.'

An interview with John the Baptist

Interviewer Do you get upset, John, when you read the Gospels?

John How do you mean?

Interviewer Well, they're all about Jesus, not you.

John Of course, they're about Jesus. They were written by followers of his.

Interviewer But Jesus was one of your followers.

John For a time, yes.

Interviewer Only for a time?

John He went his own way.

Interviewer Not your way?

John No. We had certain things in common, he and I, but not enough.

Interviewer But he came to you, out there in the desert, beside the Jordan.

John Yes.

Interviewer And you baptized him with the others?

John Just like the others, yes.

Interviewer *Just* like the others?

John Yes. The meaning of it didn't emerge till much later. Not till after his death, and after we saw him trailing the glory of God with those marks of crucifixion upon him. Extraordinary, that was. Mind blowing, soul blowing, you might say. We called it his 'resurrection'. It was ours, also.

—26—

Interviewer	*You* saw him after his resurrection?
John	Of course. I was in heaven, and he was at the centre of it all.
Interviewer	Why were you out there in the desert, beside the Jordan?
John	Why do you think?
Interviewer	I don't know.
John	What does it remind you of?
Interviewer	In the ancient tales?
John	Yes.
Interviewer	You mean the coming out of Egypt into the Sinai desert, and the crossing of the Jordan into the Promised Land?
John	Exactly that. The beginnings of freedom for the people of God; the beginnings of dignity; a land of their own, not someone else's; an end to slavery; the defeat of oppression and oppressors.
Interviewer	But why did you baptize them? The story speaks of God's making a path of dry ground across the Red Sea, and later the people crossing the Jordan without getting so much as their toes wet. You submerged people in the waters of the river, plunged them deep beneath its surface. What was your purpose?
John	To make them clean, to make them pure. If the land was to be pure again and free from oppression, then it needed a pure people, a people who had left behind in the waters of the Jordan their desire to lord it over each other. We had all had enough of people lording it over us, whether they were Romans or Herods or High Priests.
Interviewer	So you were starting a freedom movement?
John	Of a kind. God's kind, I thought.

Interviewer And that is why Jesus came to join you?

John I guess so. We both had visions of what the people of God might become.

Interviewer But he left you to go his own way. Why did he do that?

John Because our visions were not the same, neither our visions of God and his kingdom, nor our visions of his people. I thought that once enough people had joined me down beside the Jordan, there in the desert, away from the centres of power in Jerusalem, Caesarea and Tiberias, then God would come in vengeance to sweep away the impure and destroy the oppressor, and give us the freedom to enjoy his land once more.

Interviewer And he didn't come?

John Not like that at any rate. But that's not why Jesus went his own way. He didn't believe in a God of vengeance. His God was a God of outrageous for-giveness. He stopped on his way through Jericho to ask Zacchaeus if he could stay the night with him, did Jesus. Zacchaeus was one of the most hated and feared men in the town, in the region around it, and for good reason, too. He lived and worked for the occupying power and got fat on the proceeds. And Jesus asked to stay the night with him! I would not have done that. I would have shaken him out of his sycamore tree into the fires of God. We saw God differently, Jesus and I. I changed, of course, when I saw him with those terrible scars of the cross on him. That changed everything. But I had not met that God before. No-one had.

Interviewer   And you and Jesus had different ideas about the new people of God?

John   Yes. I thought they needed to be clean, washed, pure. I thought that's what holiness meant. He thought it meant sitting down with absolutely anyone and sharing your food with them and eating their food and telling stories round the circle and laughing till you fell over and not putting up with those who got in the way of the generosity of God. He didn't seem to care a fig for purity, not as I imagined it, at any rate.

Interviewer   But he still came to be baptized by you?

John   Yes. I've explained it already. Both of us had had enough of people lording it over us, I mean over our families and our neighbours, our villages and our country. We both wanted this to be God's land again, and God's kingdom. Only my notions of God's rule were too close to theirs, the ideas of our lords and masters. They had destroyed too much, too many, and I preached a God who would come with roaring vengeance and do to them what they had done to us, only much worse. Jesus' vision of the kingdom of God was quite different, as I have said.

Interviewer   And your movement collapsed, while his grew in strength?

John   Oh, I still have my followers . . . millions of them, alas, people who pray to this empty god of vengeance, and who suppose they belong to the exclusive company of the clean and the pure and wish most fiercely to keep it that way. I changed. When I met Jesus after his resurrection and found his God and knew the warmth of her embrace, I

—29—

changed. How could I not? But some still cannot see the marks on God's hands or feet, nor have ever heard her laugh. That is a tragedy... Do not follow me. My day is over. Follow Jesus instead. His day is eternal.

THE KINGDOM OF GOD

I preached this piece one Sunday at our main Eucharist in Chester Cathedral, when a small child was being baptized. It makes reference to many passages in the Gospels, as well as to Ezekiel's fine vision of water flowing from the Temple in Jerusalem, to bring life and healing to the desert and to the Dead Sea (Ezekiel 47.1–12).

You came, O Christ,
bearing questions.
You came to the Herods of your world,
to the Caesars and the High Priests
asking each of them this:
'What would your kingdom be like
if it were God's?
How would your fine kingdom be,
your great empire,
your shiny new temple,
if God inhabited your throne?
Would the hungry be fed with more than they
    could eat,
twelve baskets needed for the scraps?
Would the waters flow from your temple,
  Mr High Priest, Sir,
enough to water the whole earth
and make the Dead Sea live?
Would you sit on the floor with your women and
  your slaves, Herod,

and share your food with them,
and laugh and tell stories to one another?
Would you take a child, O great and mighty Caesar,
a small child,
and dress her in your purple robe,
set your golden laurel round her head,
not for a laugh, for mockery,
but in all seriousness?
Would you see to it, High Priest,
that no widow left the precincts of your temple
without a penny to her name?
Would you give away your shirt, Herod,
to anyone who took your coat
to keep away the winter's cold?
Would you bring healing to the sick, Caesar,
without any thought for your glory,
or descend into the stinking darkness of the prison
with new forgiveness in your hands?'

You came, O Christ,
bearing questions.
Yet you did not go to the end of the corridors of
    power to ask them;
you did not smile urbanely
as you reclined in the High Priest's dining room,
as you ate Herod's splendid food,
or lifted your glass of rare wine to Caesar,
fussed over by his slaves,
entertained by his women,
slipping your questions into polite conversation
or drunken, groping laughter.
They would not have let you through their gates,
never mind into the splendours of their inner sancta.

'What would your kingdom be like
if it were God's?'
To those who had their kingdoms
the question was put indirectly
in the crying of a baby in Bethlehem;
in the wondering of a boy in Nazareth
whether there would be any food on the table
    that night;
in a man's picturing God
as a peasant woman searching under her
    cooking pots,
as a shepherd from the village stumbling through
    the dark
with a sheep across his shoulders,
as an old man running to embrace his son.

You asked the question, O Christ,
when you faced a madman among the tombs,
or let a bleeding woman stop you in your tracks,
when you gave such honour to a woman by
    a filthy well,
to a thug in a sycamore tree,
when you refused to condemn the guilty,
or exclude the excluded;
when you came to the house of God,
found him shut in the cupboard under the stairs
and broke down the door.
You asked the question
as the soldiers beat you,
as you hung upon the piercing nails:
'What would your kingdom be like,
if it were God's?'

That was why they killed you,
because you asked that question,
in a manner they could not ignore.

And now you ask the question again
with your same urgency,
as disconcerting as ever.

Yet we will try to hear it and to understand.
We will try to follow where it leads,
where you lead, O Christ,
and we will start by putting a small child centre stage
in this grand place of yours,
for your attention and our honouring,
and we will kneel together side by side,
all distinctions done away,
and stretch out our hands,
never mind how worn or smooth they are,
to receive a taste of heaven.

Let these actions be our first answers to your question,
and let them never be our last.

WE THINK IT ALL TOO EASY
FOR YOU, GOD

Several pieces in this book make reference to the Parables of the Lost Sheep and the Lost Coin in Luke 15.4–6 and 8–9. This one is entirely devoted to them.

We think it all too easy for you, God,
I mean this shepherding of yours,
or your searching high and low
like a lonely, over-anxious housewife.
It's only one sheep, for God's sake,
when there are plenty of others;
only one blessed coin,
and still nine others to adorn your neck.

We have too much for a start,
too many things
to feel the magnitude of loss,
the beating heart,
the sudden fear.
When almost all you have
is held in ten coins,
then it is different.
We are laden with too many things
to put ourselves in your poor woman's shoes
– if she has any shoes, that is –
too many to feel her horror
when she hears the familiar tinkling sound,
the gentle pressure of the coins

unfamiliar, out of tune, too light.
Then the hurried loosening of the thread
and the counting
and counting again,
and the coming out all wrong.

For another thing, God,
we are not used
to imagining you as a peasant woman,
nor ourselves as your adornment.
We find it hard to think,
impossible, to be honest,
that we could be so rare and precious to you,
or as intimate,
or that you should go to such great trouble
    over us,
as if we're all you have!
Such divine absurdity!

We have our pride, too, as well, of course.
We do not like to be likened to a smelly sheep,
caught in a thicket by its horns,
unable to free ourselves,
trembling cold,
bleating helplessly,
alone in the dark . . .
soon the desert lions will find us,
and in the morning vultures will come to pick
    us clean.

And then we hear you,
calling our name,
calling, calling,

your voice bouncing off the sides of the wadi,
pricking the ears of the sleeping ibex;
we feel soft trembling in the ground
as your footfall comes near,
at last your hands upon us,
and no cursing us,
no cursing,
no sacrifice this time to save a son,
but easing, lifting, straining,
till we are riding on your shoulders
back to the heavenly village
and the warmth of the sheep pens.

And let us not think that journey is too easy
    for you, God,
for the side of the wadi is steep,
and first, like Christopher, you must cross
    the torrent
that roars in its depths,
where darkness is complete
and light of moon and stars can't reach;
and we have strayed far too far for our own good,
so you have a long walk back to the village,
with us draped all the way about your neck
almost as heavy as a beam of wood designed
    for crucifixion.

When finally you bring us home,
yet more surprise and more delight:
a party,
in our honour,
in the dead of night,
all heaven woken up

and tumbled from their beds,
as if your tiredness is quite gone
and we are all you have.

And we are all you have.
That is not true, of course.
And yet you take us back as if it were,
our Shepherd and our Housewife God,
and never do you count the cost.

10

I CANNOT DROWN

Set me as a seal upon your heart,
as a seal upon your arm;
for love is strong as death,
as unrelenting as the grave.
Its tongues are flames,
a fierce and holy blaze.
Even the waters of chaos,
the monstrous deep itself
can never drown it.

(Song of Songs 8.6–7a)

*This is a meditation on those lines and on the Parable of the
Lost Coin in Luke 15.8–9.*

I wished you to hang me about your neck,
as you lie upon mine,
you, my lost coin and found,
fastened tight where you belong
against the shining of my skin
so I could show you to the angels.

You did not need a rope to hang me by.
A seal is a little thing;
you would have hardly noticed my weight;
no pressure on the neck
to make you bow your head;
a thin light cord would have sufficed.

There I could have stayed
against the beating of your heart,
a small piece of earth's beauty,
carved with the intricacies of heaven,
bearing your identity,
to put your stamp on all you do
and all you are,
and my stamp, also.
I would have lain hidden there
beneath the veil of your clothing,
warmed by your warmth,
precious, cherished, held,
as I wear you against my neck.

But you pulled back your arm
and flung me to the waters,
turned your back
and let me sink,
to give me not another thought.

I know those waters well,
their darkness and their crushing weight,
for I have trod their depths before.
I cannot drown.

I cannot drown beneath your wars,
you cannot crush me 'neath the tank tracks
    of your pride,
nor strap me to your waist
and blow me up to your own kingdom come.
And even though you tie me to a cross,
and pull and stretch me to your fear,
you cannot break me,

though you turn the very sun to black
and make the angels weep.

You cannot drown my song of love
among the yelling, cheering crowds.
You cannot fly me as your precious flag,
nor pin me to your swelling breast.
You cannot make me to your own design,
nor to the fervent liking of the mob.
You cannot have me for your own;
nor will you make me hate.

And yet my necklace is too light without you.
That is still my truth.
Still I would be held by you,
and counted precious.
I will fit quite easily within your hand.
I am no millstone, after all.
Only God.

AT PEACE WITH GOD

We have peace with God through our Lord Jesus Christ.
<small>(Romans 5.1)</small>

*This piece takes that verse from Romans as its starting point,
but derives its inspiration from the Parable of the Prodigal Son
and George Herbert's exquisite poem, 'Love bade me welcome'.*

What can it mean
to have such peace with God?

It is hard enough
to have peace with ourselves,
to live with the damage done to us,
to face the truth we know,
let alone the truth that hides itself
deep within the recesses of our minds.
We can be too afraid of ourselves to be at peace,
too angry with ourselves,
or too disappointed.

Then from outside ourselves
enough presses hard upon us,
and rings its din upon our ears.

So, surely, having peace with *God*
is quite beyond us.

Indeed it is.
Thank God it's not beyond God!

For God has never been against us,
has never seen us as a threat,
or thought us a disappointment,
even when we have so cruelly disappointed.
Though we have sometimes caused God such pain,
he has never been at odds with us,
even when we have been at odds with him.

For God has always known our goodness,
and found it a source of fascination,
enough to fill the hours of heaven;
God has always known what we might be,
the good we might become.

And rejection is outside God's nature,
a divine impossibility,
thank God!

We insist on clothing God in such fine dignity,
yet he flings it off,
casts it to the winds,
and unencumbered
runs to meet us,
to fall upon our necks
and kiss us on both cheeks,
to stain our collars with his tears,
to put his rings upon our fingers
and angels' robes upon our limbs,
to sit us down before the feast of heaven
in highest place

(except that all his tables are quite round
and set in circles of equal glory).

And if we object that this is all too much,
too far from our deserving,
then God says, 'Quite so,'
and disappears into the kitchen,
beyond the swinging door,
to fetch the pud the angels have prepared
('new life by chocolate' it is called).

And so there are but these small things
required of us:
to allow ourselves to be embraced,
to sit down at God's table,
to accept the honour awarded us,
to take the gift as gift and given;
not to argue any more,
nor insist on striving for our own perfection
and God's acceptance.

Which all can be so hard, of course.

Does it help if we recall
that God offers more than acceptance,
but pleasure, laughter and delight,
bright wrapped in peace,
and holds them plain for all to see
in darkly pierced and outstretched hands?

A SAFE PLACE

A meditation on the Garden of Eden story in Genesis 2—3, and on John 10.1–15.

When we were small,
new made from the ground
or from another's side,
you put us in a safe place, dear God.

The trees of Eden bending low with fruit,
kept famine out of our vocabulary,
and drought was quite unthinkable,
for the waters of the garden
were enough to irrigate the earth.
There was work for us to do,
but toil had not yet been invented.
The animals were for playing with,
not for being hunted by.
We only saw the lion's teeth when it yawned,
heard it purr, but never roar.
The snake had no venom on its fangs,
only cleverness.
No guns thumped in Eden,
no tanks rolled,
no helicopters whirred
to make us wet our beds.

You did not mean that we should know such things.
The garden of your planting had enough for us to find
for the time being.

You would have wished, perhaps,
for that time-being to be prolonged,
stretched out to all eternity,
at least till we had gained some more maturity.
But we took the wrong fruit;
we left alone the Tree of Life,
and grabbed at knowledge of a larger world instead.

Then it was we heard the tanks coming,
and lost our childhood.

So now we live as sheep
penned in folds against the perils of the night,
with walls not always high enough
to keep out thieves and bandits,
nor stout enough to resist the bulldozer.
Eden is lost for ever.
We *know* now.

So where, dear God, might we find safety?

ᖇᖇ

'In the familiarity and the intimacy of my voice,
and the risking of my freedom.

'I made you once my children.
Now you have grown,
I call you friends.

Other shepherds call across the walls enfolding you,
promising lush pasture and sweet water,
but they do not know you as I do,
nor love you as I do.
They serve their own purposes.

'When you hear my voice,
you will not mistake it or deny.
It stirs so deep within the soul,
strikes such a chord,
conjures up such ancient, half-forgotten memories,
excites such dreams,
voices so much hope!

'Yet its echoes are soft,
embraced by silence immense,
mystery far beyond all fathoming,
and paradox of eternal fascination.

'And this I ask,
who else can call you each by name?

'Come with me from your cramped pens,
and I will lead you down to streams
that never cease their flow,
to grass that never withers in the sun,
nor dies against the winter's cold.

'And when the lionesses drop down
and slowly gather every muscle for the kill,
or when the wolves run lightly
from the shadows of the rocks,
then I will save you from their harm,

give them my blood for yours,
my flesh for them to gather round and eat,
so they will also have their eucharist.

'I cannot take you back to Eden.
For you have seen and heard too much,
and now there is too little play
and too much danger in its place.
Yet I can pour my wine and oil
upon the wounds of your knowing.
I can show you beauty beyond your dreaming,
and give you freedom there
that none can take away,
nor slam behind locked doors.
And if you are not ready for my adventuring,
then I will carry you,
until you have the strength to walk beside me.

'And one thing you did not know in Eden,
when you took that fruit before your time
– or else, in growing up so fast,
you forgot what once you knew –
I mean how very precious you are to me.
You are my gold, my frankincense and myrrh,
the flowers about my head,
the jewels upon my hand!

'And I can call you each by name.
Remember that.

'I know . . .
and still I love.'

13 AT THE GATE OF HEAVEN

Yet more use made, at the end of this piece, of the Parable of the Prodigal Son and of George Herbert's poem, 'Love bade me welcome'.

'So what's all this?' the stranger said.

The man on the gate puffed out his chest, and flicked the fringes of his epaulettes. 'This, sir,' he replied, 'is heaven.'

'Goodness me!' said the stranger. 'I had no idea.' He paused. 'It sounds a bit empty.'

'Well, we can't let in the riff-raff, sir.'

'Do these walls go all the way round?'

'Yes, sir.'

'And these are the only gates?'

'Yes, sir.'

'A bit pearly, aren't they?'

'God likes them like that, sir.'

'Oh, does he! Well, well. I never knew God was a cockney.'

'Pardon, sir?'

'What does God have to do with this place, anyway?'

The man on the gate shook his head and looked at the figure in front of him as if he was completely stupid. 'God lives here, sir,' he said, spelling out the words as clearly as he could. 'This is heaven, sir, the heavenly city, where God has his throne, sir, and his angels and all that, sir.'

'Heavens above!' the stranger cried. 'I mean, goodness gracious! Well I never! Can I have a look?'

'A look, sir? What do you mean, a look?'

'Can I come in and have a peep? I'd like to see this god of yours.'

'That would be most irregular, sir.'

'Don't worry. I won't stay. Just a quick look and then I'll get the hell out of here – in a manner of speaking, you understand.'

'Sorry, sir. Not allowed. Against the rules.'

'Whose rules?'

'Well, God's. Must be. The rules have always been here, and rules is rules.'

'I won't do any harm. Just a quick peep.'

'But you might escape, sir.'

'A quick look and then I'll come back outside. I promise.'

'Well, I don't know. I suppose you could slip in for just a second. Don't you take advantage, mind, and don't you go telling anyone about it, either. This isn't a theme park and I don't want busloads turning up. You realize I'm putting my job on the line for you, sir.'

'Are you really?'

'I've told you already, sir. I can't let anyone in. Just the people God approves of.'

'Only people. No lions, then, or hamsters, no baobab trees, buttercups, sparrows, fish eagles, dolphins, or sticklebacks?'

'No, sir.'

'No sloths specially for the sabbath, no kangaroos or king-fishers?'

'This is a city, sir, the heavenly city. When did you last see a kangaroo in the High Street, sir?'

'Oh dear,' said the stranger. 'And this is heaven, you say?'

'Yes, sir. As I said, the heavenly city.'

'Where God lives?'

'Yes, sir. As I've already explained, sir.'

'I'd better have a look at this god of yours.'

The gatekeeper opened one of the gates just enough for the stranger to squeeze through. He found himself looking up a long straight street paved with gold and glistening with diamonds. It led to a huge shining throne, surrounded by a vast crowd of adoring angels, all singing an adoring song.

'But where is everyone?' the stranger asked. 'I can't see anyone at all, just lots of rather peculiar looking angels singing a very peculiar song.'

'Well, it's true it's a long time since I let anyone in, sir,' the gatekeeper called from outside. 'In fact, I can't remember the last time. Come to think of it, I can't remember the first time, either. It's very difficult being good enough for God, sir.'

'But where *is* God?'

'On the throne, sir.'

'I can't see her.'

'You mean him, sir.'

'The throne's empty.'

'Don't be silly, sir. Can't be.'

'But it is! Look!'

The gatekeeper pushed the gates wide open. He gasped in amazement, then sat down quickly on the gatekeeper's seat. 'Oh my word!' he cried. 'Dear oh dear! Goodness me! I don't know what to think. I mean, it doesn't make any sense. Oh dear oh dear oh dear.'

The stranger sat down beside him, waited a while and then said quietly, 'I could take you to God, my friend.'

'What do you mean?'

'Have you ever met her?'

'Him, sir. Well, yes, it's true, all the time I've been gatekeeper here, I've never actually met him, or seen him. I've always thought he didn't bother with the likes of me. Too busy being Almighty and all that.

'But I don't understand,' he continued. 'I thought this was where God was. That's why no-one was allowed in, so the angels' song couldn't be spoiled, because only they know how to sing it properly and God's very particular, doesn't like anyone out of tune or behind the beat, wants everything perfect.' He turned to the stranger. 'Do you mean I've been wasting my time here?'

'And your eternity, my friend. Come with me. It's my turn to show you something now. You can ride on my back.'

'Pardon me?'

The stranger unfurled a pair of iridescent wings. The light that shone from them turned the gold of the city to brass and its diamonds to glass.

'Stone me!' the gatekeeper whispered.

'No stonings where I come from!' the angel laughed. 'Climb on my back and enjoy the ride!'

He spread his huge wings and lifted from the ground with the gatekeeper clinging on like grim death. They rose in broad circles, higher and higher, till at last the gatekeeper dared open his eyes and look down. How small the heavenly city seemed! Soon it was little more than a dot and then disappeared altogether, as if it had never been.

As they flew on, it seemed to the gatekeeper that they crossed the boundary of a new world, and soon he felt a new energy in the wings beneath him, a new buoyancy and freedom, another purpose. Before they had flown much further the angel started displaying, half folding his wings, diving down steeply, then swinging up again, turning on his back, then diving, twisting, spiralling, soaring, swooping. The gatekeeper was not afraid any more. His eyes tight shut again against the rushing air, he was enjoying himself hugely.

'Weehee!' he yelled.

Beneath him he heard a merry laugh. His angel landed

right in the middle of it. The gatekeeper jumped lightly to the ground, and before he had any time to look around he felt God's arms about him, her tears of joy upon his neck, her finest robe upon his limbs, her divine ring circling his finger and new sandals on his feet. He caught the smell of cooking in the air.

'Gabriel always gets a bit over-excited when he brings someone to me,' God said, laughing. 'Welcome, my friend. You look wonderful! My robe suits you perfectly! I've been waiting a long time for you. You must have been very lonely up there. The feast is nearly ready. Your elder brother is waiting for you, and everyone else. The sloths are hanging from the baobab trees and the kingfishers are playing with the kangaroos, as you would expect. Take my hand. Let me show you to your place, the place of highest honour, of course, like every other creature's place. And then I'll leave you for a moment while I get something out of the oven. It's a bit special.'

'It always is,' Gabriel added.

'And after we've eaten, and finished the speeches in your honour and all the songs and poems and dances, and I've done my stand-up . . .'

The gatekeeper looked at Gabriel. 'God does *stand-up*?'

'Of course,' said Gabriel. 'New material every time. That'll make your wings grow, I promise you!'

'Then,' God continued, 'Gabriel and I will teach you to fly and you will know at last what freedom means, and love, also. Come my friend, we must join the others, or dinner will be spoiled.'

A MAN WITH A LIMP

There is in Genesis 32.23–32 one of the most mysterious and profound stories in all Scripture, one in which Jacob finds himself at the wadi Jabbok wrestling through the dark hours of the night with God. It is written in Hebrew prose, but it is closer to poetry. I have been fascinated by it for years, but this meditation represents my first attempt to preach on it in what I call 'short lines'. In the course of my piece I refer back to the story of Esau selling his birthright in Genesis 25.29–34, to the tale of Jacob's humiliation of him and their father, Isaac, in Genesis 27, to the earlier parts of Genesis 32, and to the inspiring story in Genesis 33 of the reunion of the two brothers.

He was expecting to be attacked,
fearing, almost knowing
he would die.
Twenty years since he had seen his brother;
no word of him in all that time.
Now he was coming to meet him,
so his spies had told him.
With four hundred men.
They had told him that, too.
A veritable army,
and he defenceless,
with only his old trickery
up his rich embroidered sleeve
and his God . . .
but this time could they save him?

Four hundred men,
they had said.

Twenty years ago
the air in those parts
had cracked apart
with hatred and with fear.
He had tricked his brother,
his dying father, also,
humiliated them,
robbed them of honour,
dignity and blessings,
taken them for himself.
Yet they had slipped through his fingers
and twenty years had passed to find some again.
Now he was a rich man,
but would his riches help him now?

Four hundred men . . .
Open to bribery, he hoped,
his only hope.
Prayer, to be sure,
yet dare not rely on that alone.
Bribery would speak more loudly,
he thought, he hoped, he feared.
A bowl of lentil stew had done it once.
Now his brother's favour came more expensive:
two hundred she-goats, twenty kids;
two hundred ewes and twenty rams;
camels, cows, bulls, she-asses, colts,
many servants bending low . . .
throw in wives and children for good measure!
Might be enough

to change his brother's mind and heart.
They had been fickle once.
Might be so again.
He did not really trust they would.
Too much had taken place,
with too much hurt
and too much broken pride.

And so he thought he still would be attacked
by four hundred men
and a brother sore from ancient wounds.

Little did he know
that Esau trailed bright clouds of forgiveness,
and held a heart as large as heaven,
and brought a brother's tears of joy.
Little did he know he would run to meet him,
embrace him,
fall upon his neck
and kiss him.
The father of the Prodigal Son would do those things,
precisely,
but Jacob did not know that, either.

Once across the Jabbok
there was no turning back.
He knew that, all right.

And so, he hesitated.
With the Jabbok in flash flood,
threatening to sweep him away,
he hesitated.
Heedless of his wives, his children, slaves and animals

and their need of his protection,
forgetting they lay in the path of a brother out
      for revenge
(or so he thought)
with four hundred men,
he hesitated.

The water was reaching higher by the second,
faster, stronger, more insistent.
Jump into it now,
now,
and it would take him away for ever.
Esau would never find him.
He braced himself,
closed his eyes,
took a last breath of the dark air . . .

when God seized him.

He had been expecting
a knife through the throat,
not a God begging for mercy,
nor a new name,
a new identity,
nor a blessing,
not tricked for this time,
not won by two falls and two submissions,
but given with both hands
just when he thought he had lost it,
given when the mystery of it all had begun to dawn,
given when the sky was taking on the colours of
      a new day,
given when it was no longer night,

given without price,
without any further demand,
only with a limp.

What did he tell Rachel and Leah and the children?
That he had stumbled crossing the wadi
and twisted an ankle?
Yet he had no swelling for them to see,
nor pain to hear,
and the limp did not lessen as the days went by.
The way he walked
as Esau ran to meet him,
the way he walked till his dying day,
told that God had seized him,
kept him from the swirling waters,
held him tight till the night had gone,
until he knew the old trickery would not work,
until he could hear new words of blessing
and take in their surprise,
held him tight till he could set him free.

And how did God depart that place?
And had Jacob felt at any stage
the gash upon God's side,
or put his fingers into marks of nails upon the hands,
or found the holes that went right through his feet?
And was the limp only Jacob's?

THE GREATER SILENCE

In 2001 a party of us from Chester Cathedral went on pilgrimage to the Sinai desert. We celebrated the Eucharist on the top of Mount Sinai, and watched on our way back down the mountain as a flock of several thousand white storks rose on the thermals and passed us by. We lunched with the Bedouin every day. The tribes were very small, and because they tended to marry within the tribe, or with very few others, there was an eight per cent incidence of deafness among them. All the children, whether deaf or not, grew up learning signing as one of their languages.

In Exodus 2.21 we hear of Moses marrying Zipporah, the daughter of a nomadic priest who pastures his flocks in the area around Mount Sinai. There is nothing about her being deaf, but I have made her so in this story. That is a mark both of the deep impression the Bedouin made on me, and also of the freedom with which I have handled the biblical text. Indeed, I have turned Moses and Zipporah into contemporary pilgrims, who know the story of the slaughter at Jericho in Joshua 6, and have an inkling of the dangers to be found in Bethlehem, whether it be Herod's Bethlehem at the time of the birth of Jesus, or the Bethlehem of today.

My other pilgrims in this story, as I have briefly characterized them, bear no relation to the Cathedral party.

So they went by camel, at least as far as the camels could go. Moses said he was not up to climbing the direct path any more. Mount Sinai was thrust by volcanic fires tall and sheer above the desert floor. A casual glance, a second look might make you think it could not be climbed without rope and crampon. Yet there was a path of rough steps that went straight up to the summit. It was hard going, and would have been so in the cool of an English autumn day. In the heat of the desert it was more difficult still, except for the slim Bedouin, who never seemed to break into a sweat, and who belonged to that landscape and had the grace and vitality for it. Yet even they eventually became too old for the stepped path.

So they went by camel, rocking in the narrow Bedouin saddles along the track that snaked its way over the gentler, rounded slopes that lay behind the mountain's crags.

Moses was not alone this time. Bedouin children ran ahead of him, their small, bare feet caring nothing for the sharpness of the ground. His wife Zipporah came too, daughter of a Bedouin priest, dressed from head to toe in black, richly embroidered in red and yellow, and jangling with jewellery that flashed in the sun.

She came from those parts. She had taken the sheep and goats out on those mountains as a small girl, had known where water was to be found, where the most succulent plants grew, where the coolest shade could be found. She shut her eyes as the camel made its way higher and higher. The silence of the desert was immense, but Zipporah's silence was of a different kind, for like many of her tribe Zipporah was deaf. When she had married Moses she had taught him to sign, so they had always spoken to one another with their hands, their fingers, their faces, their bodies, rather than their tongues. Yet she still knew, this deaf woman, and had known it since she was a child, that behind her own private silence lay a much greater one, the silence that held the whole desert in its embrace and spoke insistently of God. She, the deaf woman, had taught Moses to listen.

She, also, was too old for the direct path, and so they went by camel, together with the scampering children; together with the man who had loved another man and been loved by him for twenty years and had never told another soul; with the woman whose husband had left her for a younger man; with the man who had worked so hard he had never seen his children grow up, and now did not know what to say to them; with the old woman whose father had so abused her; with the man whose cancer they had declared untreatable, and the old woman who lived inside her head. Only a young couple, newly married, went on foot with the children, each of them thinking of a time when they might have sons and daughters of their own, but not saying anything about it to one another.

The camels could not go the whole way. The point came when the track met the surging crags and stopped. The animals folded themselves to their knees, and slowly, helping one another, the pilgrims slid themselves to the ground. From there the path was narrow and steep. Single file they went, steps taken one at a time, the final few hundreds of feet.

Moses and Zipporah were the last to arrive on the narrow summit. They sank down on the rock facing one another. The others were already festooned here and there, sitting or standing, looking and listening. No-one spoke.

'Can you hear it?' Zipporah signed to Moses.

'Yes,' he signed back.

The silence lay as far as one could see. Along the horizon the Red Sea stretched a thin silver line. Moses' eyes turned in that direction and filled with tears. Zipporah put her hand on his.

'Look, here she comes!'

It was one of the children. She was pointing towards the south.

Moses had become very short-sighted. 'Is it God?' he signed.

'Yes,' Zipporah replied.

'Tell me, show me.'

A shimmering white cloud was approaching the mountain. Wings were riding the desert air, wings weaving with wings as they rose on the tall thermals, catching the sun as they turned, wings passing wings, spiralling upwards until they touched heaven, then gliding on in a slow descending line of grace. Zipporah signed it all to her husband, her face alive, her eyes dancing.

'The Spirit of God?' he signed to her.

'Yes.'

'I can feel her presence.'

'Of course, my dear.'

'Almost touch her.'

'Yes.'

'What about the others?'

'Oh, yes, they can, too.'

He paused. 'No more Jerichos?'

'No more Jerichos.' She looked away, her eyes unsteady.

'No more stepping over dead bodies, to take possession of promised lands?'

'No more stepping over bodies.' She wanted to reassure him and spare him pain. He had seen more than enough. Yet it is impossible to lie when using sign language. Moses did not miss the uncertainty in her eyes, but pretended he had.

'Just God, pure and simple?' he signed.

'Just God.'

'The children saw her first.'

'They often do.'

'The air is full of her beauty.'

'I know. So are these mountains, and these people.'

'And the camels.'

'Of course.'

Their busy fingers stopped and their hands dropped into their laps. They sat there not moving for a long time, the children too, and all the others.

At last Moses got shakily to his feet. He signed again to Zipporah: 'Which way was she going?'

'Towards Bethlehem.'

'I thought so.'

He walked away from his wife a few paces and looked out over the desert, a blur to him of browns and reds. It was as if his sight cleared for a moment. In the far distance he saw the shining cloud of wings. 'What will you find in Bethlehem, I wonder?' he said quietly.

GOD TREADS SOFTLY HERE

This piece was not written for Chester Cathedral, nor indeed for a service in any church, but for the vastness of the Sinai desert, and for a time of quiet we kept one day during our pilgrimage in 2001, when our Muslim guide found a place where we could sit and absorb the huge silence. I dared to break it with these few words. They draw on the same experiences as the last piece in this collection, and make reference also to Exodus 3—4 and the story of the Burning Bush, to Exodus 19ff. and the tale of God's appearance on Mount Sinai and Moses climbing to the summit to receive the Torah, to God's telling Moses in Exodus 33 that he will hide him in a cleft of the rock and pass him by, and to the stories in the Gospels of the birth, death and resurrection of Jesus.

The 'local finch' of the mountain is the Sinai rosefinch. The head, underparts and rump of the male are a strawberry pink colour. The piece bears brief reference also to my catching a tiny bird, which had got trapped one morning in the dining room of our hotel. I cupped it in my hands and released it outside. It was so small I felt no weight at all.

God treads softly here.

You do not hear her coming.
she does not mark her sacred home
with noise of thunder, earthquake, trumpet blast.
On top of ancient Sinai
her silence rests upon the world,

her words half whispered in a silken breeze.
And when she passes all her glory by,
we see her cloud of wheeling birds,
and catch her ease and grace
slipping on the desert air;
we see her wings white shining in the sun,
and watch her weaving patterns in the sky,
but yet there is no call, no cry,
no beat of wing
to break the silence of the place.

God treads softly here.

And did she really have so much to say,
when Moses toiled up there
among the sculpted rocks?
Did she drown out the local finch,
and make him blush to strawberry pink
for daring to disturb her speech?
And did her wisdom cost her reams of words,
or did she whisper in another breeze
and only lightly move the air?
And was it men who turned such gentleness,
such self-effacing, shy disturbances,
into thunder, quake and trumpet blast
of rampant religion?
And did they take the fire
that burned without the merest sound
in desiccated desert thorn,
and turn it into fearful blaze?
And should we not recall

that God treads softly here?

God treads softly here.
We hear her in the silences, both large and small;
we see her in the shadows
cast by distant birds
upon the surface of the sky;
we hold her in our hands,
and feel not even lightness there.

And so we marvel at her great simplicity,
and wonder why
we should now make her all
so complicated and confused.

The wise men came to Bethlehem
by following a thread of silent light
that led them to a sleeping child.
And though we tried to drown that quiet
by hammering the child to twisted wood,
and pushing thorns into his scalp,
yet in the quietness of the dawn,
without a sound,
without a single movement of the air,
he slipped out of death,
left his grave-clothes on the side,
and went to play his whooping games
with astonished and familiar angels.

Yet though heaven may resound to his eternal play,
God still treads softly here.
Listen!

JOB'S WIFE

The book of Job in the Old Testament, an extended poem of astonishing depth and power, tells of a man who loses everything except his wife and his tongue, and who accuses God of tearing him to pieces. Eventually God appears to him in a whirlwind, and the vision transforms him and restores his humanity. In all this, however, Job's wife plays almost no part – just six words (in the original Hebrew) for her to say near the start of the work, and then not even a mention of her. In the third and second centuries BC Jewish commentators paid her much more attention and began to imagine her pain and anguish. In this piece I am simply following their lead.

BEFORE THE WHIRLWIND

'Do not forget me. I too have lost everything. Indeed, I have lost more than my husband, Job. For he has not lost me, though I have lost him. It may be I will find him again, but for the time being I am dismissed as a fool, and not even mentioned in his fine poetry. It is as if I were not there, as if I too had died with the children, with the slaves and the sheep, or else had disappeared with the rest.

'But I have not died. I am still here, in this wretched place, with this wretched man. I bring him food and water every day. The children would have helped me, at least our daughters, but they cannot help, for they are dead. It is just me and him now, and I am as if I did not exist. I am but a whiff of smoke in the air, a stain upon the ground, a shower of rain that is gone, leaving only puddles shrinking in the sun.

'Sometimes he throws the food in my face, and smashes the water jar on the ground. And my daughters are not there to wipe me down or go again to the well. They and their brothers are dead.

'I have lost more than my husband has, for he has not lost me. I am still here. Waiting. I will be here till he dies. That day is not far away now, or so he believes. I do not know.

'It will be a mercy when he is gone. He says so himself, but the mercy he is thinking of is all for him. It will be a mercy for me, also. No more food in my face, no more water flung to the ground, no more abuse, no more watching him die.

'But what will I have then? I will have no children to look after me. I have no children. My children are all dead. The animals are gone. The slaves are gone, except four of them who are broken to pieces like the water jars. "You have your health," you say. "Not a loathsome sore on your body. You have not lost more than your husband has. How can you say such a thing? Just look at the state of him!" you say.

'Do you think I do not see it? Do you think I do not see him, this wretched man I love so, whom I cannot get near to comfort? It is not that I am beaten back by his stench. He will not let me love him. I must do everything for him at arm's length. And if you really wish to know the state of my health, then look beneath my skin, and you will see I am all rotten with grief . . . What will happen to me when Job is gone?

'I wish I had his energy, his passion. All those fine words flung into the face of God, or into the void of heaven! All those protestations of innocence! I cannot find the strength for them. He should have protested my innocence, too. For I do not deserve this any more than he does. No-one deserves the death of their children.'

AFTER THE WHIRLWIND

'Job, my love, you silly old fool, take my arm. Our eyes are too full of visions to see the potholes in the road, and our ears are too full of God's singing words to hear any danger coming.

'We can leave this rubbish heap now, turn our backs on its rotting carcasses, and shake our noses free of its stink. You smell of heaven, my love, and so do I! We have seen such things, you and I, such things! The storm has gone, yet still our feet hardly touch the ground! It will be a while before we come down to earth again, but this time we will have a gentle landing. We will not find the earth as it was before. For now we know it is of God's cherishing, born of her delight, carried on her hip, cradled in her broad lap, to be given its freedom, still in her most meticulous care.

'We had no idea she loved us so, did we, Job. Enough to make us weep, my darling. Our tears are different now.'

GETTING TO THE FRONT OF
THE QUEUE

I preached this piece in Chester Cathedral, when the Gospel set for that Sunday was the story of the Syrophoenician Woman in Mark 7.24–30. In preparation for the sermon I had read Sharon Ringe's 'A Gentile Woman's Story Revisited: Rereading Mark 7.24–31a', in A Feminist Companion to Mark, *edited by Amy-Jill Levine (published in 2001 by Sheffield Academic Press). Her article had made me see Mark's story in a new light, and it inspired me to write my sermon in story form.*

'Rich bitch,' they called me.

I'm not surprised. I was rich after all, and at their expense. They thought I knew nothing about the way they lived and cared less. I lived in the city, in Tyre, and they lived in the country. I did not know what it was to be hungry. I ate my meals reclining on a couch, served by my slave girls. I was used to silver and gold and fine glass. When drought came, as it did from time to time, we never ran short of water. When famine came, we never went hungry.

They did, the ones in the villages, working the land owned by my husband. I made it my business to find out. It wasn't easy. But I could trust one or two of my husband's slaves to bring me reports. They couldn't understand why I wanted them. A lot of the peasants in the villages were Jews. That made my enquiries even more incomprehensible, but they answered my questions all the same. I wanted to know how many families there were, how many children they had, how many of their women died in childbirth, how many of their children died young, before they were weaned, before they grew up. Did the children have extended bellies? How many, how often? And did their hair have that brown tinge to it, that meant they didn't have enough of the right food? What were their houses like? How did they eat their meals? Did they laugh and sing? Did the children play? What did they believe, the Jews among them? I had read their sacred texts, but I wanted to know what the Jewish religion was like in the villages, far away from Jerusalem and the Temple. Could they read or write at all? I presumed not, but I wanted to know.

I tried to imagine them. I tried to imagine what it was like to live in those villages in the heat of summer, in the occasional cold of winter, when the locusts came, when the rain did not fall, when disease struck and the children began to die.

I found that easier when my daughter became ill. She was my only child. My husband had threatened me with divorce if I did not give him a son. But no son had come. Euridice was our only child, and I loved her with a fierce and unrelenting love. I nearly died when I gave her birth, and that made her more precious still. She was my comfort, my light, my sun, my moon, my stars, my very life.

I had been sending medicines to the villages. I had got them from my doctors in the city, and my husband's slaves had taken them with them when they went there on his business. The villagers didn't know that I sent them. I told the slaves to keep quiet on the subject. Now I needed the doctors myself and all the help they could give, for my daughter, Euridice.

She was only five. They tried everything, but it did no good. She cried all the time, and sometimes shook uncontrollably. People said she was possessed by a demon, and that was why she wasn't getting better. I believed it myself.

I felt so helpless. It seemed that Euridice would be killed by this demon of hers. She was getting worse all the time. One day she started screaming, and when she had finished, she went strangely quiet. I was frantic, wild with fear.

Then Trycho, one of the slaves who had just come back from the villages, told me there was a Jewish healer staying in one of them. Jesus from Nazareth, he was.

'Nazareth,' I said, 'where's that? Never heard of it.'

'It's a tiny place, my lady, somewhere in Galilee, apparently,' he replied.

'Is he a good man? Good enough to drive out a demon like this one?'

'I don't know, but people are telling all sorts of stories about him.'

'But we're not Jews. Will that matter?'

'Don't think so,' he said. 'Least, they told me he'd driven a whole legion of demons out of a man living among some tombs, and that man wasn't a Jew.'

'Do you know exactly where to find him?'

'Yes.'

'Will you come with me?'

'What, now, my lady?'

'Of course. There's no time to wait. It may already be too late.'

And so we set out together, just the two of us, as fast as we could. We didn't say anything to one another on the way. Not a word.

We reached the fields near the village where the healer was. I had put on my plainest cloak, and wrapped it round my head. I wanted to be as inconspicuous as possible. But it didn't work. The men and women in the fields stopped as we approached and stared at us. Or rather, they stared at me. They knew Trycho well enough, but they'd never seen a woman with him. They guessed who I was. The way I walked, the colour of my face, the quality of my cloak.

'Rich bitch,' they called me. They didn't shout it out. Said it softly, when I was close enough to hear.

But I hardly heard them. All I could think of was getting to the house where the healer was. We passed the village rubbish heap. Three dogs were digging there for something to eat.

The children gave us a great welcome in the village. They came running out from between the houses, shouting their hello's. Their mothers told them to be quiet and shooed them indoors.

We turned left up a narrow track between some houses. Then Trycho stopped in front of one of them. 'This is where he's staying,' he said. He called out. Without waiting for any reply I rushed in through the door. The room was dark, but I saw him at once and fell at his feet. 'Euridice, my little daughter,' I said, 'She's desperately ill. She's dying. A demon, a terrible demon has got her. You must come, come now, or she will die. You can cast the demon out of her. No-one else can. But you can. I know you can. Please.'

'And what about these others?' came the reply.

I raised my head. The healer was not alone in the room. It was crowded with people, broken people, people who were used to waiting at the end of the line and never reaching the front. I had not seen them, or even guessed they could be there.

'They call you, "that rich bitch",' the healer said quietly. 'Is it fair to take the food out of the mouths of these children and throw it to the dogs?'

I looked at the people sitting in that room. I looked at their faces, into their eyes. I saw what we had done to them. I saw the dignity they were beginning to acquire as they sat with this healer, who came from a village like theirs and knew them better than they knew themselves. I had sent my medicines, hoping they would be of some help. But I had not come to their village before. It had been impossible. I was not their master, after all, nor his servant. This healer had put them at the front of the queue. He was the first person they had ever met from outside the village who had done that.

I could not drag him away from them, these people whom he loved with such a fierce love and who so loved him. He did not need to come with me to heal my daughter. He would only need to see Euridice in his mind's eye, and say the word.

I looked up at him. 'We eat at tables where I come from,' I said. 'And we have pet dogs. They wait under the tables to catch the scraps of food the children drop.'

He looked at me and smiled. His eyes were shining and his silence filled the room. At last he said, 'Your little daughter's demon has gone. Go home as quickly as you can, and you will find Euridice well. Come again to this village, and bring her with you. You will love the people here, and they will soon come to love you.'

I held his feet and kissed them, and he bent over and held me. I kissed all the feet in that room before I left, marking them all over with my lips and my tears.

The healer called to me as I was going out of the door. 'Tell your husband to come here,' he said, 'to see things for himself.'

'I will,' I cried, and ran.

When Trycho and I got home, it was just as the healer had said it would be.

The man from Nazareth had not just healed Euridice. He had healed me also, and not just of my fear.

GOING TO JERUSALEM

> Then one of the leaders of the synagogue named Jairus
> came and . . . fell at his feet and begged him repeatedly, 'My
> little daughter is at the point of death . . .'
>
> (Mark 5.22–23a)

I'd felt uneasy in their company at first. I'd been a ruler of the
synagogue in my town, and they were peasants, or dispossessed
peasants: people too often not sure where their next meal was
coming from; people living in an occupied country, like me,
but much closer to the brutalities of a Roman 'peace'; people
living beside the border and that hideous wall of destitution;
people too often acquainted with the death of their children,
or children too often burying their parents; people having to
contend with supernatural powers as well as earthly ones, for
demons were among their masters, and were the cruellest of
the lot, too.

I didn't belong to them. Not till my daughter became so
very ill, when I knew their frequent desperation. I fell at his
feet and begged him to come and heal her. But instead of
running home with me, he stopped to heal that Leah woman
who shouldn't have been on the street, in such a crowd, at all.
As if she were more important than me and my Rachel! This
wretched woman had touched his clothes, but he entirely
ignored her impurity. 'My daughter,' he called her. 'And what
about *my* daughter?' I said, but he didn't seem to hear me.
He wanted to sit down, for suddenly he felt as weak as water,
he said, just like that poor woman had felt for twelve years, he

said. All the power had gone out of him, he said. But now Leah would be like the Queen of Sheba, he said. 'And what about my little princess?' I shouted, but he still seemed not to hear, not until they came and told us she was dead. Then he looked me in the eye, and told me I had found the kingdom of God. I didn't know what he meant, not till he took my Rachel by the hand, not till we joined his followers, our whole family, not till we ate with him.

We found ourselves in company we would never have kept normally. He made no distinction between any of us. It didn't matter whether you were a man or a woman, a child or an adult, a peasant or a man like me, a slave or a free person, a Gentile or a Jew. He treated us all the same, and gave us the same food. *He* gave it to us. Didn't leave it to the women. He did the woman's work. None of us had known anything like it.

But I still wondered whether we would fit, whether we would ever be accepted. So he asked us whether we still thought the Rachels of this world were more important than the Leahs. He didn't really have to ask. He'd brought all of us back to life, after all. 'Well then,' he said, 'you fit!' And he laughed and put his arms about us and kissed us on both cheeks, each one of us. And then he said to us, 'Will you go down with me and the others to Jerusalem, for the Passover? Because it's time we all went back to Eden, to lie about in the shade of the Tree of Life, and stretch up and pick its fruit, and fill our bellies with it, and spill its waters down our chins! We've all had too much of this ancient toil. It's time we all met with God in his Garden and enjoyed his famous hospitality!'

That's what he said. How can you refuse an invitation like that? In any case we didn't need one. We would have gone with him to the end of the world and back, and so would all the rest.

So we set off with Leah and Legion and the others. He told the blind they were going to the thick darkness where God was. They told him they were already there, and he laughed, and said, 'Yes, but just you wait!' He signed to the deaf and told them they would find the same silence as Moses and Elijah had found on Sinai, and they signed back to say would God ask them what the hell they doing there, like he'd done with Elijah, and he laughed again and said, no, they would see God face to face, like Moses. He told the children that God's garden was the very best place to play in, and taught them a nonsense song for the journey. One widow woman was worried because she only had two small copper coins left, and asked him whether that would be enough. He told her she would have so much to take home with her, she would have to buy a donkey to carry it.

He meant it, of course, every word. That great pilgrimage to Jerusalem was to be the culmination of everything he had taught, everything he had done, everything he had lived. Galilee would come to God's temple. We would step across God's threshold, and sit with him and eat our fill. There would be baskets of food left over. And God would take his lyre down from his tent peg, carefully tune its strings, and play and sing to us. And we would learn his songs, and go home singing them. We would learn to sing as beautifully as the birds. Well, almost. That's what he said.

'Does God live in a tent, then?' a child asked, 'like the people in the desert?'

'Of course he does,' he replied, 'the most beautiful tent you ever could see!'

But he didn't live in a tent. Not in Jerusalem. In the Sinai, perhaps. But not in Jerusalem. They were building a huge place for him, out of great blocks of stone and cartloads of gold. And visiting God there turned out to be an expensive business. The old woman with her two copper coins was left with nothing at all. The blind and the deaf were jostled about and told they were not allowed near him. Leah and Rachel and my wife Rebekah and all the other women were told they might pollute his presence if they came too close. And the children were treated as if they weren't there, or told abruptly that playing was inappropriate. The whole place was looked down upon by Roman soldiers, and Legion nearly went mad at the sight of them, because of what they'd done to him and his family and his village up in Galilee.

Jesus did go mad. He went berserk. I'd never seen him like it. He threw their precious temple money on to the ground, set free the doves they were selling, and stopped them carrying the holy vessels about. He was disrupting *everything*.

But not for long. The temple authorities didn't need to call the soldiers. They came running as soon as they saw what he was doing. They took him away and dealt with him. We were driven out and told to go back to Galilee.

Not long after that we found God's garden there, back in Galilee, where it had all started. But that's another story.

God does live in a tent, you know. Don't try to spoil him. If you do, you will miss his great simplicity.

THE CENTURION

Now when the centurion, who stood facing him, saw that in this way he breathed his last, he said, 'Truly this man was God's Son!'

(Mark 15.39)

In a sense the whole Gospel of Mark has been building up to that statement. That it should come from the centurion overseeing Jesus' crucifixion is utterly astonishing, as many have remarked. And so I wish to interrogate this soldier, and against the background of Mark's version of the Passion, in particular his story of the soldiers mocking and beating Jesus in 15.16–20, and then his account of the crucifixion itself in 15.25–37, where Jesus first cries, 'My God, my God, why have you forsaken me?', and then gives a second 'loud cry' as he dies.

'We know so little about you. You leave us with many more questions than answers. Yet one thing we know about you is so extraordinary that we cannot forget you. We mean the words you spoke beneath the cross, "Truly this man was God's Son." That is six words. But Mark wrote in Greek. In his Greek it comes to seven. Collecting together the cries of the dying Jesus from the four Gospels, we often speak of "The Seven Words from the Cross". Yours are "The Seven Words beneath the Cross". We will ask you in a moment what it was you saw that brought such a speech from your lips.

'But first we wish to know about this business of crucifying. You were the officer in charge that day, ordered to make an example of a troublemaker who had nearly set the whole city ablaze with his antics in the Temple. How many men had you hung on crosses before? We used to have public executions in this country, too. You, an officer in the army of an occupying power, must have seen many of them, performed many of them. Did you have it down to a fine art? Were you an expert at turning the screw of pain? Were you brutalized by it all, as torturers generally are? You took this particular prisoner, Jesus from Nazareth, outside the walls of the city, to a piece of cracked rock on the edge of a disused quarry, above a rubbish dump. You took especial care to insult him and his people. Was that your idea? Or were you only obeying orders? We do not suppose you had much say in the matter, till it came to the flogging and the hanging and the intricacies of its performance. But tell us, did you relish it? Did the adrenalin flow? Or did you have to get yourself drunk to find the stomach for it? Your men seemed to enjoy themselves when they beat him half senseless, and dressed him up in royal purple, and crowned his head with stabbing pain, and bent the knee. They had a rare old time. Did you join in? Did you start it all? Or did you just stand and watch as they indulged themselves?

'Was that, by any chance, when first he caught your eye? Did you kneel, yourself, at his feet, and suddenly find that kneeling was appropriate? Did you begin to have your doubts then, not just about his innocence, but about the meaning of what you were doing? Did you hide such thoughts as these from your men, from yourself, maybe? Or were you lost in the routine of your cruelty, noticing nothing?

'You saw something when he died. We can be sure of that. Why else should you speak those extraordinary words? They were the words of God, you know, spoken at baptism and at transfiguration, *his* baptism and transfiguration. Twice

God broke his silence and spoke out the truth. "You are my Son, the one I love," he said, as the Jordan water cooled his sides; "This is my Son, the one I love," he cried to Peter, James and John, when suddenly they found themselves caught in the circle of the divine.

'What did you see to make you speak with the voice of God? You had heard the man shout he felt abandoned by God, and with another shout he died. What was in that second cry? Was it more desolation? Or was it love? Whatever it was, it made you turn and look.

'And then you saw. Standing beneath the gibbet your men had arranged so skilfully, you found yourself in the shadow of God, and realized it was God's loneliness you had heard, God's own near despair. And surely, whatever that second cry was, that final thrust of lungs against the nails, you knew it carried all the ancient love of God. That must have been what made you start. That was when you knew this was no routine execution, but the turning point of the world, and that after this things would never be the same.

'What then did you do? You told Pilate the man was dead. Mark tells us that, also. You answered his straightforward question. Did you tell him the rest? If you did, then Pilate took no heed.

'And that is how your story ends. We know nothing more of you. You leave us with so many questions, and yet still with that startling statement of the truth. For that we will never forget you.'

21   MARY OF MAGDALA

I preached this piece in Chester Cathedral on the Feast of Mary of Magdala. It is a meditation on the famous story in John 20 of Mary's meeting with the risen Jesus, though it borrows the detail of her bringing spices to the tomb from the Gospels of Mark and Luke. I am indebted to Mark Stibbe, in his Sheffield Academic Press commentary on John, for drawing my attention to the passage from the Song of Songs.

> Upon my couch at night
> I sought the one I love –
> I sought, but found him not.
> 'I must rise and roam the town,
> through the streets and through the squares;
> I must seek the one I love.'
> I sought but found him not.
> I met the watchmen
> who patrol the town.
> 'Have you seen the one I love?'
> Scarcely had I passed them
> when I found the one I love.
> I held him fast, I would not let him go.

> (Song of Songs 3.1–3; the translation is taken from
> the Tanakh, a modern Jewish translation of what
> we Christians call the Old Testament)

Two women searching in the dark,
each of them distracted by desire
for the one they love.

The first is searching for the living,
and wants him in her bed;
perfumed, she knows her scent will entice him;
finding, she knows him at once,
does not need to question him,
holds him fast and will not let him go.
No mistaking him
for a street-sweeper,
no needing her name to be called.
She has no name for us to call her by,
she sheds no tears,
all ends in joy.

The second searches for the dead,
her perfume not upon her skin,
but held tight in her hands
for the staunching of the stink of death.
Out of her mind with grief,
she finds the body gone.
Loss is piled on loss, it seems
and she is broken-hearted twice.
Twice she has mislaid him,
this one she loves,
for death removed him from her sight,
and now the gardener has done the same,
or so she thinks.

She cannot bear it,
falls into wild words of 'taking him away'.
How will she carry him?
Where will she take him?
She makes no sense,
though all her love is true.

He is, the one she loves, far more elusive
than that other man,
that unnamed man of city streets and squares.
This one, though he has a name, cannot be grasped
   at all.
What is he doing out of the bed of his tomb
on a cold morning,
without the wrappings of his burial?
What is he doing out of *death*?
It makes no sense –
unless, of course,
he happens to be God.

Is that the reason why she does not mark his form,
although she sees him, stands so close,
addresses him, accuses him almost –
because he happens to be God?
And is that why she cannot hold him,
because he happens to be God,
and God eludes us always,
escaping us in order to be God?
And is that why he calls her name,
and only needs that one small word,
to pierce her grief
and turn it all to joy?

For with this 'Mary!'
all spins round to joy,
the deep, transforming joy
of finding God
and knowing him for who he is,
her friend and her companion,

her teacher, healer
and her love.

Now we too must set out in the dead of night.

A MILLION NIGHTINGALES
AND THE SCENT OF HEAVEN

There were also women looking on from a distance; among
them was Mary of Magdala . . .

(Mark 15.40)

*I have put this piece in Mary's mouth, making reference as I go
along to the song that Jonah sings from the belly of the fish in
Jonah 2. All four Gospels speak of Jesus being buried by Joseph
of Arimathea. But just suppose it happened differently . . .*

Let me tell you another version of the story. You will not
like it.

That business of Joseph of Arimathea and the tomb in the
garden, and the spices for embalming his body . . . it didn't
happen like that. We wanted to pretend it did. We wanted
to pretend he'd finally been treated with some kindness, even
if it had come too late. We wanted to pretend we'd done
something, that there had been something for us to do. He
had been robbed of all dignity, all humanity on that cross.
You wouldn't do that to an animal. For the soldiers he was
nothing, his execution just a job to be done, to be sworn over.

His burial was the same. The soldiers did it. That's the
truth. No prayers, no lamentation, no ceremony at all. Just
more cursing and swearing, the digging of shallow pits, the
humping of bodies, the retreating of marching feet. At least
they didn't leave him to the wild animals and the vultures.

The soldiers are usually the last to leave the scene. But I hid
myself in the shadows when they left Golgotha, and went and

stood beside the little mound of earth where my good friend now lay, his body not yet cold. The patch of ground beneath his cross was dark with his blood.

The night came, and I was still there. Was it a dream I had? I don't remember sleeping. How could I have slept on that spot, after what had taken place there? Was it a vision then? That seems the best word for it. The soldiers had left a ladder behind, leaning on one of the arms of his cross. They'd used it when they'd got him down. They knew they would need it there the next day, I suppose. Of a sudden it seemed to me that its top reached to heaven, that heaven had come to earth. And then the ancient firmament broke apart, and the world was flooded once more, to wash its violence away, only this time it was flooded by the waters of God's love.

I recalled that ridiculous song Jonah sang from the belly of the fish, and in my dream, my vision, call it what you will, I sang it to the right words:

> I called to the Lord out of my distress,
> and he answered me.
> You have cast me into the deep,
> into the heart of the seas,
> and your flood surrounds me.
> Your mercy has closed in over me,
> the depths of your forgiveness surround me,
> and all your love is wrapped about my head.
> All the world is drowned in your love!

As I sang, the power of Rome seemed very small. The nakedness of the emperor was clear for all to see, and Pilate's, too. The soldiers had seemed to be in charge on that hill, but their brutality was now exposed as an empty sham, pathetic posturing!

In the middle of that dark night the sun rose, and the mockery and curses of the soldiers were replaced by the singing of birds, as if all the birds of the world were in that place, declaring it the territory of the God who had made them. And the shallow graves were covered with flowers. Would the birds' song reach the ears of Pilate? Would the emperor come from Rome and pick these flowers? Oh, I hoped so! I cried out with a loud voice. 'Come and listen!' I shouted. 'There are a million nightingales here! Bend down and smell these flowers! They are bursting the air with the scent of heaven! Come, take off your shoes, for this is a holy place, this is holy ground, for this is God's dancing floor! Come, take my hand, and let us dance this night away, and let us shake the ground till Rome and all the world's Romes tremble!'

It can't have been a dream. At least I must really have shouted. For the next thing I heard was a soldier's voice. 'What the hell are you doing here?' it said. I felt a soldier's hand grip my arm.

But the birds kept singing. I can still hear them. I can still smell the flowers, too. And I can still hear that voice. Another word was spoken from the cross that day, though no-one else has mentioned it. I heard it quite clearly, as the flood of God's love broke noiselessly upon the world and overwhelmed me. 'Mary,' he said. That was all.

It brought me to my senses, and made me raise my head to catch the full light of that strange rising sun. For I had heard that voice before, many times. It was the voice of Galilee. It was the voice of God.

A GOD WITH A
GALILEAN ACCENT

Another piece put in the mouth of a rather feisty Mary of Magdala. Unlike the last, it accepts the story of the Gospels that Jesus was buried in a proper tomb, particularly John's version of it in 19.38–42, and it turns again to John's beautiful story of her meeting with the risen Jesus. It also speaks of the Garden of Eden story in Genesis 2—3, of the book of Job, both of the intervention of Job's wife in 2.9–10, and of the imagery and metaphors used in the first speech of God in chapters 38–39, and of the story of the Burning Bush in Exodus 3.

Do you remember Job's wife? She came to her husband in his agony, filled to the brim with her own grief, and asked him, 'Why do you cling so tightly to your precious piety? Speak out the truth! Curse God and die!' And do you remember how he dismissed her? 'You talk just like one of those foolish women,' he said. What he meant was, 'Typical woman! Women never see sense. Wisdom and insight are the preserve of men, and good theology, too, of course. Women are left with their intuition, but everyone knows that can't be trusted.' That's what he meant.

And that's why you think me a foolish woman for not recognizing my risen friend, when I met him in the garden beside the entrance to his tomb. I was blinded by a woman's tears, you say. 'There you were,' you say, 'looking straight at him, and you mistook him for the old man digging up the weeds!' But I can easily be forgiven for the mistake, you say. As if it needs forgiving, and as if, in the first place, it was a mistake.

Because it wasn't. I was not mistaken. It was my moment of recognition. You think that came later, with the calling of my name. But I had already grasped the truth by then and already been astonished.

Let me take you back to another story, back much further even than Job, the story of a place called Eden, where we and the animals first emerged, creatures of God's finger and thumb. 'And the Lord God planted a garden in Eden,' this ancient story says. 'Planted a garden', it says. It's easy to miss those words, because we can hardly believe them. For our God has lived in a palace for millennia, in a city, in a heavenly city, in heaven, behind walls built too high for the wicked to see over, and pearly gates plastered with notices about rules of admission. We have made God too high and almighty for such a thing as gardening, his hands too clean, his mind too fixed on higher things. And men whose hands have never been calloused and their nails always clean, and who have pretended their minds are fixed on higher things, have made sure God has been kept like that. Yet that's what the story says. He 'planted a garden'. 'Ah yes,' you reply, 'but he wouldn't have done it himself. He would have got the angels to do the job. He would have taken the credit, of course, but he wouldn't have done the work himself. God doesn't do that sort of thing.'

But he does, you see. Jesus, the carpenter from Nazareth, taught me so. We sat together one morning on one of the hills overlooking the Sea of Galilee, surrounded by its wild profusion of flowers and its wheeling birds, and he told me of the God who appeared to Job and his wife in the whirlwind (it was always Job and his wife with Jesus), the God who built the foundations of the world, the God who digs irrigation channels in the desert, the God who helps the ibex and the gazelles give birth to their young. And so, you see, when I hear in the story of Eden about God planting a garden, I'm not a bit surprised.

My surprise, on that morning, on that first day of the week, in that garden of the tombs, was finding myself so suddenly in the presence of God, and recognizing his face. Perhaps you cannot come upon God gradually. Perhaps God is always a surprise. Certainly I was not expecting him. I was not expecting anything. There was nothing I could do, after all. I couldn't even anoint my friend's body, for Joseph of Arimathea and Nicodemus had already done that, with an absurd amount of myrrh and aloes, as if he were a pharaoh waiting for a pyramid. I wouldn't have done all that. But I would have done what I could. They had left me with nothing to do. I went back all the same. I wanted to cling on to him, I suppose. I couldn't let him go, not just like that. Golgotha had been so noisy. The quietness of death, even his death, would come as a relief and give me space to cry.

So I went back as soon as I could, and found myself all of a sudden on holy ground. The rising sun was shining through a bush of thorns, and turning it to fire, and immediately I took off my shoes, just like Moses. The holiness of the spot took me by the throat. I could not hear a sound. It was utterly still, as if the whole world were holding its breath. And I held mine, forgetting to breathe. Then I saw him, and I heard his voice, and I let out a cry. For I recognized him. It was the Gardener, the one who had planted Eden. I didn't need telling that. I knew him at once. When you meet God face to face, you don't need to be introduced. But I don't mean that. I recognized the face. I knew the voice. This God spoke with a Galilean accent, and bore the features of my Galilean friend!

THE PATRON SAINT OF THOSE
WHO MAKE MISTAKES

*A piece first written for a Eucharist in Chester Cathedral on
the Feast of Matthias, whose story Luke tells in Acts 1.15–26.*

You were an afterthought, Matthias,
taken from the substitutes' bench
because a member of the team had let the side down,
had died the death of an evil man
and gone to hell as he deserved,
or so the rumours said.
(Your teacher, Matthias,
your companion, your friend,
the one who showed you God,
had spoken of forgiving enemies,
had acted out forgiveness on a cross,
had cried at the dark centre of his agony,
'Father forgive them; they know not what they do.'
But those words were quickly forgotten, it seems,
left behind in lonely utterance,
hanging in the fetid air of crucifixion,
and absent from an upstairs room,
where lots were cast
and you were chosen.
And so the Master of Forgiveness,
the one who'd harrowed hell,
was compelled to return
to search for Judas
among the rubble he had left before.
We must make our God so weary sometimes!)

You are the patron saint, Matthias,
of all who are considered afterthoughts,
living proof, it seems,
that such can be picked by God after all,
and quite as carefully
as those called by name beside a Galilean shore.

We have read the Gospels right through, Matthias,
every word,
and nowhere did we come across your name.
There are no stories told of you;
the lists of names do not contain you.
And yet you were there all the time,
we are now informed,
from the baptism of John
(as early as that!)
till his ascending day.

You then were on the lake with him;
you sat in his circle and ate with him;
you saw the shock as he told of a 'Samaritan'
walking down the street
among the people frozen to their café seats,
gripped by the fear of another bomb,
his pockets filled to bursting with oil and wine
to pour on wounded heads;
you heard him ask Zacchaeus for a meal and a
    bed for the night,
that nasty little man who so had terrorized
the good people of Jericho, and the bad,
with the deafening demands of an occupying power;
you stood beside him as he touched lepers
and sent them home;

you watched him as he brought God
to the mad and the ones no-one could reach;
witnessed, over and over again,
his outrageous forgiveness.

And we did not know,
for your story and your part in his
were left untold.

Were you there, then,
in the shadows of Gethsemane,
when the mayhem of the temple
caught up with him?
Did you, also, draw your sword,
and find the sharpness of his tongue?
Did you run away like the rest,
and leave him to the small, despairing comfort
of the women?

We do not know.
Your story and your part in his
are not told.

What did he say to you, Matthias,
in those precious moments
when the two of you were on your own,
and how did you respond?

We do not know.

You met him risen from the dead,
a God marked for eternity
by driven nails and spear.

You met heaven come to earth,
as it squeezed itself into a crowded, secret room,
fresh from Emmaus and the mischief of the
     broken bread;
and you were there to receive the blessing
of pierced, uplifted hands.

That we know.
And that is all we know.

You are the patron saint, Matthias,
of those whose stories are left untold,
the unremarked,
the unnoticed,
the ignored,
the very ones
upon whom the choice of God is set.

Or is that true, Matthias?
Were those fateful lots cast
because of a misunderstanding,
because the friends of Jesus,
and you among them,
had yet to come to terms with that cross
and all it meant?
because you still were hoping
for an Israel strong enough
to drive the Romans into the sea,
longing for a God riding the clouds
with angels poised in helicopter gunships?
because you thought you needed twelve
     new patriarchs,
to sit on thrones judging the twelve tribes

and anyone else needing your wisdom?
because you had forgotten the lessons
of the child set in the centre of the circle,
of the women paid such honour,
of the feet washed,
of the bread broken and the wine poured,
of his dying in the way he did,
of his rising with those marks upon him still,
brutality not punished,
but taken to eternity
and utterly transformed?

Did God really have new patriarchs in mind
    after that?
Did he need an inner circle any more?
Had he not made plain
how wide and far his mercy roamed?
Had he not done away with holies of holies
and their over-respected attendants?
Had he not rolled back the stone
and set his laughter free?

If that is so,
why then, Matthias,
you are the patron saint of those who make mistakes
and do not understand!

We thank you for your blessing!

ADDRESSES TO THE
MIDWIFE GOD

You are the one who drew me forth from the womb,
the one who made me safe upon my mother's breasts.
On you I was cast from my birth,
and since my mother bore me you have been my God.

(Psalm 22.9–10)

*This remarkable portrayal of God as a midwife, which occurs in
a few other places in the Old Testament, such as Psalm 71.6
and Isaiah 66.9, has long fascinated and inspired me. I decided
to draw out the metaphor and stretch it a little. This piece was
the result.*

THE MOTHER

'You were the difference between life and death, God. I would
have died without you. You delivered me. As simple as that.
Except it wasn't so simple, was it. That was the trouble. He
was the wrong way round, and my pushing got me nowhere
at all, nor him, either. Waves of pain crashing on to me to no
avail, like the waves of a dead sea. Until you put your hands
on my stomach and managed to turn him. The pain had
nearly exhausted me by then. I would have died without you.
You delivered me. Turned the child inside me towards birth,
turned my pain to good effect. It had gone on so long, I had
thought it would never end. Wave after wave, after wave. But
you delivered me, and turned my pain to joy.

'You took my child from me, the child with whom I had

struggled for so many hours, the child who had wrestled so hard to be born, you took him, cut the cord that held us together, and gave him back, no longer curled up in the dark, no longer tied to my womb, but lying for all to see upon my body, with his mouth at my breast.

'I could see the colour of his eyes and his hair! I could count his fingers and his toes! They were all there! Quite extraordinary! And when your work of delivering me was done, and all the tasks you had to perform for my new-born child, you withdrew and left me to my fine, strange, flooding joy. (I soon discovered, of course, what other floods this child could cause.)

'You were so self-effacing. In the end I forgot to thank you for saving two lives. And I forgot to thank you for your pleasure, the huge pleasure you took in my joy, the same pleasure you took in my child. You should have seen your face, dear God, when you held him! I thought, foolishly, that midwives were more detached, more used to it all. You wept as if you had never seen or held a child before. You seemed as surprised as me, as overcome, by the sheer wonder and beauty of him. Almost as if he were your own, as if you had formed him in the womb yourself, and guarded him safe there for the day of your deliverance.

'I had heard before, my God, that you delivered people. I did not realize it would be like this, nor lead to this, my child.'

THE CHILD

'I cannot find the words I want for it, my birth, I mean, or for you, God. You are quite beyond my describing. But, as you know, we babies are not so good at keeping quiet for long, so I will have my say.

'When I am more grown up than I am now, some adults

will tell me you keep your distance, and that a great gulf is fixed between us and you. Well, I shall tell them you don't, and there isn't. I felt you turning me, when I was all curled up the wrong way inside. I heard you speaking to my Mum. Or was it me you were reassuring and encouraging? Probably both of us. I was glad to hear another voice, I can tell you! My Mum sounded so exhausted, so frightened. And all I could do was suck my thumb and kick. Until you turned me and showed me the way out. You and my Mum together, you brought me out of the dark into a light I had never seen before. It had been all safe and warm in there, and it was hard leaving it behind. It nearly killed me. But then I felt your hands upon me, and the last bit was easy.

'At the moment of my birth there was nothing between us. You held me in your hands and then in your arms. You snipped the cord that had held me and been my lifeline. You set me free. Your freedom alarmed me at first. I did not want such early independence. I made my feelings heard about it, as you well know. And you were so pleased at my crying, as I took my first breaths of air and discovered how strong my lungs already were! You wept for joy. You held me for a moment to your cheek, and it was all wet with tears. It was as if I were your own child, your own son, as if you had conceived me and carried me in your own womb. You cut my umbilical cord and let me free, but you seemed absurdly attached to me, dear God. You seem so still. You will always be attached to me, and never will it make any sense.

'Then you gave me away, gave me back to my mother. And when all was well, and I had found again the warmth of my mother's body and the comfort of her breast, you slipped from the room and left us to our unique intimacy.

'I shall never forget, dear God, that larger, more ancient

intimacy of yours. It saved my life, and my Mum's. Your hands have left their mark upon me, and your tears, also. My divine birth-marks. I will carry them for the rest of my life. You will recognize me by them.'